Our society's definition of success—in w[...]
of money and power—isn't working. Wit[...]
practical tools, *Hands Free Life* offers the in[...]
our lives with more grace, more joy, more gratitude, and more love.

Arianna Huffington, author of *Thrive*

Rachel does it again! As I read *Hands Free Life*, I felt my pulse slow, my lungs fill, and my anxiety lessen. Rachel's writing is a Reset button. Her advice is practical, and her message is clear, gentle, and true: Less stress! Less distraction! MORE LOVE! Thanks, Rachel, for reminding us what matters: our people.

Glennon Doyle Melton, author of *New York
Times* bestseller *Carry On, Warrior* and founder of
Momastery.com and Together Rising

In this intensely insightful book, Rachel teaches parents how to engage with their children as they truly deserve: with heart, presence, and grace. *Hands Free Life* will inspire you to grow with your children and reach depths of your being like never before. Its words will allow you to discover your highest potential as a parent and thereby bestow your children with an inestimable gift: your engaged being.

Dr. Shefali Tsabary, *New York Times* bestselling author
of *The Conscious Parent*

If you need a clear-minded and clear-hearted guide to a more fulfilling life, this is it. Again, author Rachel Macy Stafford provides us with actionable and meaningful ways to love well, live fully, and leave a legacy we can be proud of.

Patti Digh, author of *Life is a Verb* and seven other books

Rachel's wise words inspired me to be a more connected, more present parent, and for that I'm so thankful. I'll be handing this out left and right to the people in my life.

Shauna Niequist, bestselling author of *Savor*
and *Bread and Wine*

It took one day. I only could allow one day to read *Hands Free Life*. I was busy being a dad, a husband, and a cancer patient. I knew I was distracted, but there was a purpose. I was on a mission, and I acknowledged my limited time. As I settled in to read Rachel's words, my heart stayed in my throat the entire journey. She gets it. She knows we're distracted, and it's not just the number of screens we have in our lives. It's our incredibly complex, crazy, and somewhat out-of-control lives. Rachel Macy Stafford will help you reconnect and build strong relationships. Even if you make a moderate amount of effort, your family will thank you for strengthening your relationships! Once again, I owe Rachel a big thank-you for bringing relationships and family to the forefront of everyone's mind.

Garth Callaghan, *The Napkin Notes Dad*

Reading *Hands Free Life* spoke to me at a deep, heart level. It challenged me to stop hurrying through life, quit worrying about what other people think, and start savoring the ordinary, everyday moments. I smiled through some parts, cried through others, and came away with fresh resolve to make each day count—not in more efficient productivity, but in more meaningful relationships. Highly, highly recommended!

Crystal Paine, founder of MoneySavingMom.com
and New *York Times* bestselling author
of *Say Goodbye to Survival Mode*

Rachel's words beautifully remind us of the little things—and the big things that make a LIFE. A happier, healthier, more fulfilled life. In *Hands Free Life*, we are gently but firmly guided to unplug from our 24/7 world and to passionately pursue the connectivity that is so vital to our children, partners, families, friends—and ourselves. Pick it up today—and I promise: you won't want to put it down.

Amy McCready, founder of Positive Parenting
Solutions and author of *The "Me, Me, Me" Epidemic—
A Step-by-Step Guide to Raising Capable, Grateful Kids
in an Over-Entitled World*

Can I simply say: Read this beautiful book. It will feed your soul, free your spirit, and fill your heart. *Hands Free Life* is an irresistible wake-up call for all of us who wish to parent more thoughtfully, love more generously, and live more joyously.

Katrina Kenison, author of *Mitten Strings for God*
and *The Gift of an Ordinary Day*

With her unique blend of transparent storytelling and thoughtful insight, Rachel Macy Stafford reminds us again why hers is one of the most important voices of our generation.

Joshua Becker, bestselling author of *Simplify*
and founder of *Becoming Minimalist*

Hands Free Life is the perfect combination of advice and anecdote. Stafford's personal stories are engaging and enchanting, while her daily declarations serve as their punctuation; reminders that we need to pause and let go of the chaos, ensuring our hands are free to embrace the grace in parenting's small moments.

Jessica Lahey, author of *The Gift of Failure*

Rachel has written a beautiful and profoundly wise book, one that heightens our own joy of life and enables our children to fully thrive.

Marilyn Price-Mitchell, PhD, developmental psychologist

Hands Free Life came to me right when I needed it most. Essentially a road map for intentional living, Rachel's approach, stories, and message are making a difference in my life by teaching me to grasp hold of what really matters.

Ali Edwards, storyteller and author of *Life Artist*

I was hooked from the first story. Rachel's writing is like a bear hug from a loving parent — warm, reassuring, full of joy, and a strong reminder of love and security. This book will speak to every loving parent's heart with wisdom and insight that is sure to strengthen every family.

Justin Coulson, PhD, parenting author,
researcher, speaker, and father of six

I want to give this book to every parent I know. Rachel Macy Stafford's gentle spirit and insightful wisdom leaves readers encouraged, inspired, and challenged to cultivate more intentional, present lives. I am a better mother because of *Hands Free Life.*

Jessica N. Turner, author of *The Fringe Hours*

In the midst of countless daily reminders to hurry up and catch up, does it ever feel like all you do is *mess up*? The message of *Hands Free Life* reads like a gift and a second chance. If you long to linger in your own life but aren't sure where to start, let Rachel Macy Stafford show you how. Her gentle words will cast a hopeful vision for your family, with practical tools to help you create the margin you long for and the relief your soul needs.

Emily P. Freeman, author of *Simply Tuesday:*
Small-Moment Living in a Fast-Moving World

Just a couple of chapters into *Hands Free Life*, I learned not to sit down with the book unless I had a box of tissues at the ready. Rachel's truthful style of storytelling brought me to grateful tears again and again, redirecting my gaze me back to the beauty found in my everyday, regular ordinary ... and reminding me that perfectionism is not a prerequisite for a hands free journey. Such a freeing message!

Jamie C. Martin, author of *Steady Days*
and writer at SteadyMom.com

At last — a book about changing habits that didn't leave me overwhelmed and doubtful, but rather excited and hopeful! Rachel Macy Stafford's gentle tone, personal reflections, and easy-to-embrace habits inspired and encouraged me, so much so that I found myself instantly — and naturally — incorporating her insights and ideas into my day. *Hands Free Life* is simply a must-read if you want to be lovingly guided toward filling your days with more meaningful and enjoyable moments.

Sheila McCraith, author of *Yell Less, Love More*

In today's distraction-filled culture, it's tempting to fill our days with "busyness" to feel like we're accomplishing something, while the reality is we're just moving farther and farther from the kind of authentic life we want to create. Rachel Macy Stafford's new book, *Hands Free Life* is the antidote to the hamster wheel! With compassion and empathy, this "been there, done that" mother teaches readers how to build an authentic and satisfying life that matters.

Meagan Francis, author of *The Happiest Mom*

With a refreshing focus on less pressure, more love, *Hands Free Life* beckons us to a life that cherishes the individuality of each family member and the transformative power of presence. This book is about less pressure, more love; less comparison, more perspective; less distraction, and more life!

Anna Whiston-Donaldson, *New York Times* bestselling author of *Rare Bird*

Hands Free Life is such an important book! One of biggest challenges most of us face in today's digitally connected, fast-paced world is how to disengage from technology and connect to the things and people that matter most. Rachel Macy Stafford's powerful and down-to-earth advice helps us live with more presence, awareness, and perspective.

Mike Robbins, author of *Nothing Changes Until You Do*

This book expresses what an amazing time we can have within the family dynamic when we learn to let go of the excessive demands we find ourselves in. It allows us to become aware of the way we self-talk about our parenting while promoting how to live life to its fullest in harmony. Rachel has so eloquently shared what it takes to *"keep track of life"* and how it impacts our relationships with those we love.

Lisa Hein, international bestselling author and motivational speaker

Hands Free Life is a heartwarming book by a talented writer who lifts you up with inspiration and plants your feet squarely on the ground, ready to focus on what really matters.

Sandra R. Blackard, author of *Say What You See® for Parents and Teachers*

HANDS FREE

Life

9 HABITS for OVERCOMING DISTRACTION, LIVING BETTER & LOVING MORE

RACHEL MACY STAFFORD

New York Times Bestselling Author

ZONDERVAN®

ALSO BY RACHEL MACY STAFFORD

Hands Free Mama

ZONDERVAN

Hands Free Life
Copyright © 2015 by Rachel Macy Stafford

This title is also available as a Zondervan ebook. Visit www.zondervan.com/ebooks.

Requests for information should be addressed to:
Zondervan, 3900 *Sparks Dr. SE, Grand Rapids, Michigan* 49546

Library of Congress Cataloging-in-Publication Data

Stafford, Rachel Macy, 1972 –
    Hands free life : nine habits for overcoming distraction, living better, and
loving more / Rachel Macy Stafford. – 1st [edition].
       pages   cm
      ISBN 978-0-310-33815-4 (softcover)
      1. Conduct of life. 2. Contentment. 3. Distraction (Psychology) I. Title.
BJ1589.S824 2015
248.4 – dc23   2015016159

Cover design: Juicebox Designs
Interior design: Matthew Van Zomeren

First printing June 2015 / Printed in the United States of America

Dedicated to Scott, Natalie & Avery
for providing the essentials for this journey.
Your laughter is my fuel. Your hand is my hope.
Your grace is my sustenance.
Your wisdom is my guide. Your love is my true north.
My precious ones, you are home.

CONTENTS

Introduction: Living a Life that Really Matters 11
Keeping Track of Life Manifesto 19

PART ONE: Creating Lasting Connections 21

HABIT 1: FILL THE SPACES 23

Fill the Spaces with the Songs of Life 27
Fill the Spaces with Connective Silence 32
Fill the Spaces with the Sound of Hope 36
Hands Free Life Habit Builder 1:
    Taking Off the Ticking Clock 41

HABIT 2: SURRENDER CONTROL 43

Surrender Control to Be Free of Past Mistakes 46
Surrender Control to Broaden Future Opportunities 50
Surrender Control to Fulfill Your Life's Purpose 56
Hands Free Life Habit Builder 2: Opening Clenched Fists . . 60

HABIT 3: BUILD A FOUNDATION 63

Build a Foundation through Listening 67
Build a Foundation through Lifelines 71
Build a Foundation through Faith 77
Hands Free Life Habit Builder 3: The Best Ten Minutes 81

PART TWO: Living for Today 83

HABIT 4: TAKE THE PRESSURE OFF 85

Take the Pressure Off so Others May Too 89
Take the Pressure Off to Live Life Fully 93
Take the Pressure Off to Embrace Good Enough for Today . 97
Hands Free Life Habit Builder 4: Making Today Matter 103

HABIT 5: SEE WHAT IS GOOD 105
See What Is Good to Nurture Inner Gifts. 109
See What Is Good to Gain Perspective 115
See What Is Good to Become a Noticer 120
Hands Free Life Habit Builder 5: Glimmers of Goodness . . 124

HABIT 6: GIVE WHAT MATTERS 127
Give What Matters to Play Again. 131
Give What Matters to Gift a Moment. 135
Give What Matters to Ease the Pain 140
Hands Free Life Habit Builder 6:
    Offering a Piece of Yourself. 144

PART THREE: Protecting What Matters 147
HABIT 7: ESTABLISH BOUNDARIES 149
Establish Boundaries to Protect Innocence 153
Establish Boundaries to Protect Relationships. 158
Establish Boundaries to Protect Moments. 163
Hands Free Life Habit Builder 7: Hands Free House Rules . .167

HABIT 8: LEAVE A LEGACY 169
Leave a Legacy to Grasp Simple Joys. 173
Leave a Legacy to Inspire a Future Generation 180
Leave a Legacy of Self-Kindness. 184
Hands Free Life Habit Builder 8: The Presence Pledge 187

HABIT 9: CHANGE SOMEONE'S STORY 189
Change Someone's Story by Responding with Empathy. . . .193
Change Someone's Story by Opening Your Arms. 199
Change Someone's Story by Taking the First Step 203
Hands Free Life Habit Builder 9:
    The Six-Second Challenge 208

Conclusion 211
The Ultimate Hands Free Life Habit Builder:
    If I Live to Be 100 215
Acknowledgments 217

Introduction:

LIVING A LIFE THAT REALLY MATTERS

LIKE MOST PEOPLE WHO enjoy their sleep, I'm not a fan of middle-of-the-night awakenings. Typically, I provide what is needed—a glass of water, a lost stuffed animal, or a kiss on the cheek—and then quickly usher my child back to bed.

But this particular night was different.

Maybe it was because my daughter Avery was unusually hot with fever. Or maybe it was because my Hands Free journey had taken up permanent space in my head, consistently pointing out when to pay attention. Whatever the reason, I felt compelled to crawl all the way into my child's bed and nestle under the covers when she quietly commanded, "Stay, Mama."

Once settled, I cupped Avery's round face, which still held traces of baby, and whispered, "I am here."

These three spoken words appeared to bring great comfort to my child's weary head, and her eyelids began to close. That is when I studied her face. Every eyelash. Every freckle. Every curve of her small, sweet mouth. I felt the need to soak up every detail of her six-year-old self. Although my eyes stung from a need for sleep, I felt a sense of peace knowing I was exactly where I needed to be.

Just as I was about to nod off, my daughter's eyes suddenly flew open. Had I not administered the medication myself, I would've thought she'd been given a double shot of espresso! With the skill of a seasoned news reporter, Avery began drilling me with questions—questions that even in the light of day would be challenging.

> Has anyone in our family been to war?
> What war was it?
> How did your grandparents die?
> Will I die of old age?
> Will you die of old age?
> Will Grandpa and Grandma die soon?

I managed to answer the first five questions somewhat satisfactorily given my level of alertness, but the last one stumped me. I began to stall. "Well, Grandma is hoping to be at your high school graduation, so let's see that's ..." Mumbling to myself, I began adding the number of years until my child graduates to my mother's current age.

My observant child immediately noticed I was miscalculating. "No, Mama. Grandma is seventy-three, not seventy-four," she corrected. I was about to speak, but something stopped me. I sensed Avery was not finished yet. Illuminated by a crack of white light streaming from her bedroom closet, Avery lifted her hands in front of her face. Like the wings of a bird about to take flight, she spread her small fingers as far as they could go. It was then that this child with sweat-fringed hair and flushed cheeks soberly stated, "I'm keeping track of life."

I actually stopped breathing for a moment.

Keeping track of life.

It was such a beautiful term, and one that became almost magical given the way Avery extended her two free hands. But what made the hairs stand straight up on my arms was the fact that I knew exactly what it meant. *Keeping track of life* is knowing you're on your true path toward fulfillment. It's being at peace with who you are and how you are living. It's placing your head on the pillow at night knowing you've connected with someone or something that made your heart come alive. It's investing in what really matters, understanding full well that managing life is the tendency but living life is the goal.

Keeping track of life is much more than going through the motions of putting down the phone, burning the to-do list, and letting go of perfection. It's something deep. Lasting. Permanent. It is a conscious decision to focus on what really matters when a sea of insignificance tries to pull you away.

I knew what it meant to *keep track of life* because it had become my daily practice. What began as small steps to change my distracted, perfectionistic, and hurried existence grew into a transformed perspective—one that profoundly altered the way I made decisions, interacted with my loved ones, focused my attention, and spent the precious minutes and hours of my days. Intentional actions to grasp what really mattered had evolved into living a *life* that really mattered.

Along with my hands, my eyes and heart were opened, allowing me to identify the greatest distractions of the modern age—distractions that cause people like you and me to lose track of life to the point that it seems irretrievable. Perhaps that is where you are right now, wondering if it's even possible to reclaim your life from the demands of a distracted culture and an overwhelmed life. I can assure you—it's not too late. In fact, this very moment is a beginning. The same two hands that hold the pages of this book are the very hands that can put *living* and *loving* back on the priority list.

THE POWER OF OPEN HANDS, EYES, AND HEART

By now, most of us are aware of the cost of everyday distractions. The blatant diversions of a tech-saturated, overscheduled, maxed-out world interrupt our conversations, steal our focus, and undermine our ability to be present in the moment. Using mindful strategies we can curb these obvious distractions and create a healthy balance between tech and life. But that is only half the battle. To be completely free to focus on what truly enriches our lives, we must learn to recognize the larger, all-encompassing distractions that divert our attention from our greatest goal: to live and love fully. The distractions that get in our way take many forms, but perhaps you'll relate to one of these:

Sacrificing everything to climb the corporate ladder

Striving to achieve the illusion of a perfect home and perfect life

Pushing loved ones to excel in certain areas despite their lack of interest, talent, or ability

Serving on endless committees to prove your worth

Engaging in people pleasing to gain acceptance

Seeking external validation for superficial reasons and from questionable sources

Making important life decisions based on what other people think or do

Going to dangerous extremes to maintain a certain appearance or status level

Attempting to control the uncontrollable

Acquiring the latest and greatest material possessions in order to impress

Replaying past mistakes and not allowing yourself to move forward

When we become consumed by these corrosive yet virtually unseen distractions, we stop asking questions. We fail to assess if we are on the right path toward our life's purpose. We become complacent and accept that this is just the way it is despite the emptiness and stress that keep us awake at night. Before we know it, we lose track of what matters most in life, only to later realize we've accomplished much but lived little.

We all yearn to look back on our lives to find we lived a life of significance. But is it even possible anymore? We live in a culture where grand achievements and small waistlines are complimented on a daily basis ... where busyness is a badge of honor and excess is the norm ... where electronic messages have replaced face-to-face contact ... where day-to-day responsibilities overwhelm and downtime is extinct. Considering the degree of distraction and amount of pressure that exists in the world today, *keeping track of life* may seem impossible.

But I am here to tell you it is not.

You have the power to make meaningful, lasting human connection despite the busyness of everyday life.

You have the power to live in the now despite that inner nudge pushing you out of the moment toward perfection and productivity.

You have the power to protect your most sacred relationships, as well as your values, beliefs, health, and happiness, despite the latent dangers of technology and social media.

You have the power to pursue the passions of your heart without sacrificing your job or your daily responsibilities.

You have the power to evaluate your daily choices to ensure you are investing in a life that matters to you.

Whether you are just starting your journey toward a life that really matters or have been at it awhile, my hope is that this book will help you to create life-altering habits that enable you to invest in what is most significant. As your hands, heart, and eyes become open, you will find yourself thinking differently about life. With a Hands Free Life perspective, you have the power to keep track of life so that one day you will look back and see you didn't just manage life—you actually lived it and lived it well.

HOW TO USE THIS BOOK

Through my ongoing journey to let go of distraction, perfection, and societal pressures to grasp what really matters, I have discovered nine intentional habits of a Hands Free Life. These life-changing practices make up the nine chapters of this book and fall into three parts: *Creating Lasting Connections, Living for Today,* and *Protecting What Matters.*

Drawing on insights and discoveries from my personal journey, each chapter explores one habit of a Hands Free Life. Sprinkled throughout each chapter are affirmations called *Hands Free Life Daily Declarations.* These uplifting statements are designed to inspire mindful daily practices and new thought processes to help you establish and maintain your own Hands Free Life.

Each chapter concludes with a powerful perspective shift I experienced on my journey called a *Hands Free Life Habit Builder.* These poetic reflections are intended to be something like a manifesto, a hymn, a prayer, or a meditation you can use to reinforce that particular Hands Free habit in your own life. Although much of my writing inspiration comes from my children, the discoveries in the *Hands Free Life Habit Builders* and *Daily Declarations* can be applied to all areas of life—parenting, marriage, friendship, work, family caregiving, and personal well-being.

KEEPING TRACK OF LIFE STARTS NOW

On the night of Avery's illness, she finally stopped talking and succumbed to sleep. I, on the other hand, lay wide awake, feeling grateful for the small hand that clung lovingly to mine despite my past mistakes and daily failings.

In that loving gesture, the most promising aspect of *keeping track of life* presented itself. *Keeping track of life* is not a contest; it is not a competition. There are no tally marks; there is no grading system; there are no awards. *Keeping track of life* doesn't work like that.

By the grace of God, *any* act of love and *any* offering of genuine presence—no matter how small or imperfect—counts. And what's more is that you can start *keeping track of life* anytime, anywhere, at any age—despite what happened yesterday.

In fact, you can start right now.

Push away doubts—especially the one questioning if life's too far gone to ever be retrieved.

Silence the inner critic—the one who says you are too flawed, too distracted, too damaged to ever be worthy of a fulfilling life.

Dismiss the drill sergeant, the perfectionist, the control freak, and the frantic rusher—those whose relentless demands sabotage any chance of meaningful connection in the blur of a frenzied day.

> Life is meant to be lived
> not managed,
> not controlled,
> not screamed,
> not stressed,
> not hurried,
> not guilt-ridden,
> not regretted,
> not scripted,
> not consumed by distractions, big or small, obvious or subtle.

It's time you lay your head on your pillow at night knowing you achieved something of significance—not in terms of societal standards, but in terms of the light in your child's eyes, the curve of your spouse's lips, and the beat of your very own heart.

So open your hands and spread them like a bird taking flight. With a Hands Free view, you have the power to rise above the distractions of the world and see a clear path to what matters most.

KEEPING TRACK OF LIFE MANIFESTO

← ❥ ❥ ❥ →

Not the digits on the scale
Not the numbers in my salary
Not the speed at which I respond to a text message.

Not the square footage of my home
Not the circumference of my waist
Not the number of tasks I accomplish in a day.

Not the markings on my social calendar
Not the collection of awards on my wall
Not the volume of extracurricular duties I juggle all at once.

Instead
I'm keeping track of life.

I'm making the moments count . . .
In the kisses
In the hugs
In the words of my loved ones that ease my cluttered mind.

I'm finding joy in the now . . .
In the blessings
In the do-nothing moments
In the sacred pauses of life that heal my frenzied soul.

HANDS FREE LIFE

I'm keeping track of life
By cupping it in my two free hands
Because I don't want to miss a childhood
a marriage
a friendship
or the moments that make life worth living.

I'm keeping track of life
Because now I see what's important cannot be measured,
    purchased, or checked off a list
It must be felt through the open hands and heart of an
    awakened soul.

PART ONE:

Creating Lasting Connections

Habit 1:

FILL THE SPACES

◄——— ❧ ❧ ❧ ———►

And the only thing people regret is that they didn't live boldly enough, that they didn't invest enough heart, didn't love enough. Nothing else really counts at all.

Ted Hughes

PERHAPS WHEN COMPLETING MEDICAL documents or school registration forms, you've come to three very important lines labeled *Emergency Contacts*. These blank spaces cause you to go to dark places you don't often go and ask questions you seldom want to consider. *Who could you call at 3:00 a.m.? Who could decipher your inaudible sobs? Who could you trust with your most precious gifts?*

My pen always hangs suspended over those lines. No matter how much of a hurry I am in to submit that form to waiting hands, I am always forced to pause. Those empty lines are sacred spaces and cannot be taken lightly. I didn't always have this perspective, though. It wasn't until recently, when I was pulled aside by a woman at a party, that I saw the significance of the *Emergency Contacts* spaces as they related to a Hands Free Life.

"Are you Rachel Stafford?" a woman with a familiar face asked me over the low roar of party conversation and festive music.

When I nodded, she said, "You are the emergency contact for half my preschool class."

It wasn't meant as a compliment, but as the words rolled off her tongue, I felt like she'd placed a crown on my head. I felt the magnitude of the message's meaning in a way I hadn't before.

Rachel Stafford, *Emergency Contact*

Although there are many esteemed titles in today's society, I could not think of a higher honor at that moment. I know that might sound strange. After all, we work tirelessly to have prestigious labels added to our name — PhD, PTO President, VP of Finance, Bestselling Author, Employee of the Month, and so on. But I wasn't considering the woman's comment from a mainstream point of view; I was looking at it from a Hands Free Life perspective.

And that makes all the difference.

You see, the inherent responsibilities required to inhabit the sacred space on an Emergency Contacts line — connection, trust, time, and availability — are also essential for building close relationships, which is one of the key features of a Hands Free Life. It was through Avery's desire to learn to play the ukulele at a young age that I learned both the importance and the ease of filling the sacred spaces of our days with meaningful interpersonal connection.

Not quite four years old, Avery needed my assistance whenever she practiced the new ukulele chords her instructor Mr. Andrew taught her. I clearly remember sitting beside her on our golden-yellow sofa as the late afternoon sun poured onto my lap. Being forced to focus on one thing and one thing only caused my left leg to jiggle nervously. With clenched teeth and frazzled hair, I watched in angst as my child stumbled through "Kookaburra," the first song she ever learned.

As small, uncoordinated fingers struggled to find their home, I'd eventually have to cover her fingers with my own in order for her to make a clear sound. Despite the Grand Canyon–sized lulls between each strum, I could not fold towels (I tried) or write grocery lists (I considered it) during practice sessions. For Avery to create any musical sound whatsoever, I had to *be in the moment*.

For a woman whose life was based on efficiency, productivity, checklists, and tangible results, ukulele practice was a form of slow, grueling torture. But although ukulele practice cramped my multitasking style, I did it because my daughter loved that tiny wooden instrument. And when she sang, her God-given purpose filled the room and I felt an unexplained peace within my soul.

So we kept practicing—Avery on her C chord and G chord and me on sitting still and not multitasking the moment away. We both made considerable progress relatively quickly. By the time Avery moved on to her first Taylor Swift song, the urge to get something accomplished while she practiced was completely gone. Perhaps what was even more monumental was that my mind was at rest too. I stopped thinking about a million other things and allowed myself to simply be *all there*. Avery began announcing, "Time to practice!" more and more. As much as she loved singing and strumming, she knew this was *our time*—and that was significant.

During one of our connective practice sessions, I noticed the spaces between her teeth—specifically the baby teeth gaps that are only there for a short time. Her big sister's were already gone. As Avery strummed and sang with an openmouthed smile, I blinked back tears of joy because, for the first time, I could see my child clearly. Every exquisite detail of my child that had slipped by me unnoticed before was now magnified through my new Hands Free lens. Filling small increments of time with loving presence had not only drawn my child and me closer, but my outlook on life was being transformed. As my priorities began to shift, I felt great hope that I could reclaim my life despite my previously distracted existence.

If ten minutes of daily ukulele practice could strengthen the bond between my child and me, what could happen in the ten minutes that my children spoon breakfast cereal into their mouths at the kitchen table? What could I learn about them in that three-minute wait for the bus? What could develop in the four minutes that it takes for my husband to remove his tie and dress shoes as he begins to unwind for the day? What memories could I glean from my dad's still razor-sharp mind in those forty-five minutes he sits on my back porch when he comes to visit?

Suddenly those little pockets of time that were so easily devoured in the name of productivity were viewed as opportunities to focus my undivided attention on what really mattered. Making it a daily practice to be fully present while in the company of loved ones meant the difference between intimately knowing and superficially knowing the people I love. It meant the difference between living each day catching glimpses of joy or just barely surviving each day without even a smile.

Filling the spaces, the first intentional habit of a Hands Free Life, doesn't require large amounts of time, elaborate gestures, mastering new skills, or extensive planning; it does require you to show up—heart, mind, body, and soul—when in the company of those you love. In this chapter, we'll explore three ways you can fill the spaces of everyday life with loving intention. It is my hope that you discover, as I have, that regardless of your occupation, past history, or current life challenges, creating deep and lasting connection *is* possible.

Whether we are talking about the Emergency Contacts lines of an official document or drawing closer to another human being, the critical element needed to fill the sacred spaces is the willingness to be *all there*. Being someone who shows up consistently in everyday life or one who shows up in a time of need are both traits of a life well lived. After all, it's not the prestigious title behind our name or type of car parked in front of our house that gives meaning to our lives—it's knowing we didn't miss the gaps in the teeth or the lyrics of our life.

FILL THE SPACES WITH THE SONGS OF LIFE

For a culture that prides itself on immediate results and instant gratification, it may seem strange that we are also experts at putting off living—the best parts of living. "When I drop a pant size …," "When things at work slow down …, " "When schedule isn't so crazy …," "When I get that promotion …" are just a few of the twenty-first-century ambitions that keep us from taking a break, having fun, and connecting with the ones we love. But this type of procrastination comes at a great cost: the opportunities of today are lost in that delay of truly living.

Although we've been led to believe that our fondest memories are made in the grand occasions of life, in reality, they happen when we pause in the ordinary, mundane moments of a busy day. The most meaningful life experiences don't happen in the "when," they happen in the "now." This concept is not earth shattering, nor is it something you don't already know. Yet we still continually put off the best aspects of living until the conditions are right. But what happens when we continually put productivity above investing in relationships?

One day I decided to find out.

As a personal research project to fuel my writing, I spent a few hours compiling every email message I'd ever received from individuals who wished they could turn back time. I simply typed the word *regret* in my subject search and with that, I hit the mother lode. I read the messages one by one—real stories of real people with wishes that could never come true.

I wish I hadn't spent so much time working.
I wish I'd spent more time getting to know my kids.
I wish I'd developed a relationship with my sister when I had the chance.
I wish I would have forgiven my mom a lot sooner.
I wish I would've said, "I'm sorry" once in a while.
I wish I would've said, "I love you" every chance I had.

Although we are inundated with the advice to "cherish every moment" to the point that it sounds meaningless, something powerful happens when you read the regrets of real people with real names and real pain. Their heartbreaking truths wake you up.

And that's exactly the state I was in this particular evening; I was fully awake to the preciousness of time. And it just so happened that I had the rare treat of being alone in the car with my ten-year-old daughter, Natalie. We were coming back from an outing, just the two of us. I was taking the curves of a meandering country road at the pace of a leisurely Sunday drive. The sun was setting and we were talking.

In the midst of a discussion on how to pass a driver's test, Natalie heard the first three notes of her latest favorite song faintly drifting from the car speakers. "Turn it up, Mom. I love this song!" she exclaimed.

Natalie immediately began singing without restraint—as if she was alone in the car. As if no one else's opinion mattered. As if she suddenly discovered the liberating freedom that comes with open windows on a warm summer night.

I couldn't believe what I was hearing—this was my computer whiz, my studious planner, my competitive swimmer, my baker extraordinaire. I would fully expect this musical outburst from my ukulele-playing younger daughter, but not Natalie! I couldn't remember the last time Natalie sang uninhibitedly like this—perhaps when she was three or four years old.

Looking in the rearview mirror at that moment was like looking into a crystal ball. Suddenly I could see Natalie at age sixteen: a burst of colorful style bounding into the kitchen—the scent of teenage grooming quickly overpowering the smell of bacon and eggs. I envisioned her nails, cut short and square with vibrant polish, grabbing the car keys. She wouldn't have time for a hot breakfast. With barely a wave, the door would shut, and I would be left in eerie silence wondering where the time had gone.

The collection of email messages I'd gathered earlier that day prominently came to mind. With vivid detail, I saw a tangible form of Regret. It was plopped down before me like an old dog wanting a little acknowledgment, a little attention, a little respect. And it wasn't going anywhere.

With longing eyes, that old dog looked at me, and I could practically hear his persistent line of questioning. "So what are you going to do about me?" asked Regret. "What are you going to do *now* so I'm not lying at your feet *later* when your hair is silver, your hands are arthritic, and time is no longer on your side?"

Suddenly a painful commentary went through my head: I know I can't possibly cherish *every* moment. I know it's not realistic to neglect my life responsibilities to soak up every word and every expression of my family members and friends. I know that telling myself to savor every stage of childhood or every season of life is just setting myself up for failure. So what do I do? How do I realistically live life *now* to avoid the pain of regret *later*?

As I looked in the rearview mirror, my daughter's chocolate-brown eyes met my gaze. With a sudden sense of urgency, I felt opportunity staring me right in the face. *Stop thinking* what if *and sing! Sing before the song ends!* I told myself.

So I opened my mouth and joined in. Surprisingly, Natalie didn't give me an exasperated look. She didn't roll her eyes and beg me to stop. She didn't chuckle and say, "That sounds terrible, Mom!" My daughter's smile grew, and she kept right on singing.

When we walked in the house a few minutes later, it was eerily quiet. Natalie surmised that Avery was still running errands with Daddy, and it would be the perfect time to purchase a gift for her little sister's upcoming birthday.

Natalie sat down at the computer and typed in the web address of Avery's favorite store. I saw the American Girl doll site appear, and I knew my meticulous child would spend quite a bit of time carefully examining each and every item before making her decision.

I stood there a moment studying the back of Natalie's head — each strand of hair perfectly highlighted by the powerful combination of chlorine and summer sun. As much as I wanted to reach out and gently smooth her hair, I felt a pull—a pull to the dirty dishes piled in the sink ... a pull to the mess scattered around the family room from a hasty departure ... a pull to check the messages in my in-box ... a pull to check at least one task off the to-do list.

But the song is half over, I remembered.

"Can I sit with you while you look?" I asked my thrifty daughter, who'd gone straight to the sale section of the site.

"Sure, Mom," Natalie replied in a cheerful voice that indicated her face held a smile even though I could only see the back of her head.

And although looking at the American Girl doll website for almost thirty minutes wasn't the most entertaining activity ever, listening to my child carefully determine what two items her sister would love best was unforgettable. And that's when it hit me. Cherishing every moment until my child leaves home is not possible. After all, there are jobs to do, bills to pay, and deadlines to meet. There are school assignments, extracurricular activities, home duties, and volunteer duties. *But there are moments in between life's obligations when we are in the presence of our loved ones that can be made sacred.*

Meals at the table, caring for pets, walking around the block, morning send-offs, afternoon greetings, and nightly tuck-ins all hold great potential—potential to be *all there.* Within the duties of life, there are opportunities to meet her gaze in the rearview mirror ... to ask her questions ... to listen to her thoughts ... to sit beside her as she does something she enjoys ... opportunities to sing along to her favorite song ... opportunities to sing along to the music of her life.

Believe me, I could fill those opportune moments with to-dos. I was born with the ability to spot tasks that need attention every second of every day. But during my highly distracted years, I found that it doesn't take long before those lost opportunities begin to accumulate. When they start to pile up, they get heavy and the pain becomes inescapable. And farther down the road,

I imagine that pile of missed opportunities will look a lot like Regret—the kind of Regret that lays at your feet after your loved ones have gone, making you wish you could turn back time.

But this story is not about Regret. This story is about hope because there's a song playing right now. If you listen closely, you can hear it . . . you can see it . . . and you can learn to seize it.

It's a Lego creation on the floor. It's a tea party in the playroom.

It's a pickup basketball game in the driveway. It's a cozy table for two in the corner of Starbucks.

It's a wheelchair ride down a musty corridor to show feeble eyes the beauty of a summer morning.

It's a phone call to an estranged friend that begins with "I've been thinking about you . . ."

It's an apology, a white flag, an olive branch between two people who love each other very much but will never see eye to eye.

It's a lingering hug, the smoothing of a stray hair, an invitation that sounds like "What do you want to do today?"

There's a song playing right now, today. And it's not over yet. So push aside your hesitations, your duties, your distractions, and your pride for just a moment and sing along. Sing along so the people you love know that you're *all* there and there's no place else you'd rather be.

In about twenty or thirty years, let Regret be someone else's companion. Because you'll be looking back on your life with a smile on your face and a song on your lips.

HANDS FREE LIFE DAILY DECLARATION

Today I will not put that which is urgent in front of that which is important. Today I will look for opportunities staring me in the face with big brown (or blue or green) eyes. And when I see a chance to love, listen, sing, dance, laugh, or rest, I will seize it. This day could be checked off or it could be lived. I choose to use these hands, this heart, and these eyes to let it live.

FILL THE SPACES WITH CONNECTIVE SILENCE

In an especially chaotic rush out the door to go on a family vacation, I sat in the passenger seat fuming. Mad because I didn't have time to put the dishes in the dishwasher. Mad because we were late getting on the road. Mad because the garage door was acting up. I am talking trivial, insignificant, minor inconveniences here, but that was the state of a distracted woman who could no longer see the blessings, only the inconveniences, of her overscheduled life.

Just before we were about to pull out of the driveway, my husband, Scott, looked at me as if someone he loved very much had died. In a barely audible whisper he said, "You're never happy anymore."

I wanted to defend.

I wanted to excuse.

I wanted to deny.

But I couldn't.

Because I knew he was right.

Where had that cheerful woman gone? The one who smiled at people she passed on the street just because. The one who felt happy when she heard her favorite song or had a pack of strawberry Twizzlers in her purse. The one who experienced a surge of joy when she pulled the car over to watch a sunset or rescue a stranded turtle.

When I looked at the pained expression on Scott's face, I wondered how long it had been there. Just how long had I not noticed what I was losing as my hands, heart, and mind were consumed by the fleeting, superficial, and meaningless distractions of my life. I was the closest I'd ever been to society's definition of "having it all" yet the farthest I'd ever been from the life I yearned to live.

As odd as it may sound, that dark truth became a beacon of hope. You see, not too many months later, Scott and I were given the rare opportunity to get away for five days. It would be the first time in six years we'd been away from parental duties and everyday pressures for more than a day or two. It would also be the first tropical island we'd ever visited. I was determined to take Scott's painful truths and my newfound awareness and use them for good. On this vacation, I would be distraction free — not just unplugged, but completely engaged, attuned to my husband, my surroundings, and my connection-starved soul.

For added motivation, I shamefully recalled how many vacations I'd ruined by focusing on all the wrong things:

Fretting over how I looked in a swimsuit ...
Dwelling on all the things I "should" be doing in the name of productivity ...
Trying to capture the perfect photo and caption to post on social media ...
Attempting to stay current with the endless stream of information on the Internet ...
Getting upset if things didn't go according to my plan ...
Feeling like we needed to be doing something every single moment in order to have fun ...

It was no wonder the joy was gone from my face and my heart. These shallow preoccupations acted as barriers separating me from the most fulfilling aspect of life: to love and to be loved.

But not on this vacation.

I purposely brought a small suitcase so I would not be weighed down by choices and excess. Blank notebooks and pencils replaced devices and calendars. Hats and headbands replaced blow-dryers and curling irons. I squelched the compulsion to plan out our days and instead let them naturally unfold. Interestingly, Scott and I found ourselves starting each day with a long morning hike and ending our days parked in the sand watching the sun make its descent.

The woman who had become too busy to watch the breath-taking sight of another day gone by saw four consecutive sunsets. And in those hours sitting side by side in beach chairs against a backdrop of fiery hues, I learned things I didn't know about my husband of fifteen years. Scott listened to newfound dreams that I didn't have fifteen years ago. We got to know each other again — the "fifteen years later" version of the person we love even more today than we did on our wedding day.

But let me be completely honest: While it's true that Scott and I shared great conversations that were on a deeper level than they were at home, it wasn't like that every minute of the vacation. We didn't find ourselves continually conversing without a single breath in between. We weren't constantly pouring out our hearts or whispering seductively in each other's ears like over-the-top lovers in a Harlequin romance. Sometimes we just shared moments of *connective silence*. Why connective? Because in those conversation lulls, I didn't check out. I didn't reach for the phone, the television remote, or a few pages of unfinished work. For the first time in a long time, the quiet pauses of our days and nights were not marred by the noise of the outside world or the micromanager in our heads. After a few moments of quiet tranquility between Scott and me, something would eventually come to mind and one of us would speak. Sometimes it was something simple, but other times it was something profoundly meaningful.

As the vacation progressed, the silences became more comfortable and more restorative. Like a seashell tucked inside my shirt pocket, I vowed to take the following discovery back home with me: perhaps the greatest opportunity to connect to what really matters lies in the silent spaces of our day. When we resist the urge to fill every minute with noise, excess, and activity, we open the doors of our heart, mind, and soul to let the joy come in.

Near the end of our trip, Scott and I took a spontaneous eight-mile hike to the island's historic lighthouse. The rustic trail was comprised of crushed shells and ran along the exquisite shoreline. A few feet off the beaten track, I noticed some plastic red flowers sticking out of the ground. I felt compelled to investigate. As I approached, I felt as though I was about to receive a divine sign that I was on the right path toward a more meaningful life.

Lovingly surrounded by sun-bleached, weathered seashells was a headstone. The top line on the tombstone read: *In loving memory of our sunsets together.* Although it was a balmy 85 degrees that day, the words gave me chills.

Reading further, I discovered someone's dearest love had been seventy-four when she passed. I squatted down and honored her with a moment of silence. Scott's hand came to rest on my back; no words were needed. Something told me my prayer was his prayer. *Thank you, God. Through you, even the darkest truths can become beacons of light. Even the most pained expressions can be transformed to smiles. Even the most deafening silences can be the pathway to the deepest connections of the human heart.*

 ## HANDS FREE LIFE DAILY DECLARATION

Today I will seek two empty-handed moments, two complete-silence moments, and two fully available moments. I will avoid setting expectations for what is to happen during these moments. Instead, I shall allow these moments to unfold naturally so there is room for them to flourish, evolve, and transform into fuel for my connection-hungry soul.

FILL THE SPACES WITH THE SOUND OF HOPE

As the final bites of dessert were savored and dishes were cleared from the round tables, I saw the coordinator of the women's event take the stage. The women at my table smiled at me, reminding me that it was my turn. Our dinner conversation had been so enjoyable that I nearly forgot I was not simply having dinner with friends but was the keynote speaker of the evening's event.

I scooted to the edge of my chair, thinking the announcer would probably touch on a few highlights from my biography and invite me forward. But as I looked around at a sea of captivated faces, I realized she'd gone off script. In a voice heavy with emotion, the woman told the audience there was a Hands Free strategy that had changed her relationship with her child. The crowd grew silent, hanging on every word she spoke of *The Heartbeat Check,* a ritual I wrote about in the very early stages of my journey. While this was going on, I experienced two completely inappropriate reactions: first, shock. I couldn't believe someone outside my parents and their retired friends at the exercise club had been reading my blog way back then. Not only did this woman just acknowledge she'd been reading my words since the blog's inception, but she'd used my messages to create a family ritual that was still alive years later. I was shocked.

And then I was sad.

The Heartbeat Check, which had once been a great source of connection with my own children, was no longer in existence at my house.

Where had it gone?

Why did we stop?

What have I missed?

As the clapping ensued, I realized that while I was sitting there quietly falling apart, my introduction had concluded. I quickly got ahold of myself—after all, I was about to take the stage and tell a large group of people to let go of distraction, perfection, and guilt. This was hardly the time to beat myself up over lost opportunities!

I managed to compose myself and make it through the sixty-minute presentation with no other thoughts about the forgotten ritual. Afterward, I made my way over to the woman who had introduced me and told her how much her words meant to me. The woman's eyes teared up as she disclosed a few more personal details about the sacred bonding time with her daughter. Then she covered my hand with her own and thanked me for bringing her closer to her child.

As I looked into her hopeful eyes, I realized this was not a time to feel shame or regret; this was a time to be grateful for the powerful reminder I'd just been given. By choosing to look forward rather than back, I could seize this gift—I just hoped it wasn't too late.

The next evening, I initiated my plan to bring *The Heartbeat Check* back into play. I started with the most likely candidate. I crawled up next to Avery, who was cozily nestled in her lime-green comforter awaiting her nightly tuck-in. To my highly affectionate child and her gaggle of stuffed animals, I immediately fessed up. "Do you remember when we used to do *The Heartbeat Check* at bedtime?" I asked optimistically.

This child, who remembers exactly where she placed her eyeglasses in a sea of overgrown grass and the precise location of three long-gone bruises from a tricycle mishap when she was two, nodded eagerly.

"Well, last night I realized we stopped doing *The Heartbeat Check,* so I was wondering if we could start again," I said, my voice rising along with my hopes.

Instantly I was reminded why being six is so awesome. When you're six, you can *always* pick up where you left off. With no reprimand, no lecture, and absolutely no discussion whatsoever, my child abruptly peeled back her comforter to expose the panda on the front of her hot-pink pajamas. She pointed straight to the fuzzy black-and-white target and said, "Here ya go, Mama!"

I laid my head on her flannel-clad chest. Her heart sounded just as I remembered—calm, steady, strong. Fearing I may have suffered hearing loss over the past several years, my child clamped her arm around my head and pushed it closer to her beating heart. "What's it sound like?" she inquired.

I mimicked the sound I heard with a "lub-lub, lub-lub" and then added, "Your heart sounds really happy tonight. Maybe it was because you completed that Lego beach house without help or maybe it was because you tricked me into eating that sour gum and couldn't stop laughing!"

With a huge smile, Avery suggested a few more reasons why her heart was happy that night. Then she sat up abruptly and announced, "My turn!"

How could I have forgotten? With this particular child, listening to *my* heartbeat was just as important as listening to *her* heartbeat.

Suddenly a mop of unruly curls fanned my face. My cuddly child wiggled around until she got a clear sound. "Your heart sounds like this: Boom, badoom, boom ... Boom, badoom, boom."

Hmmm ... my heartbeat sounded eerily similar to the chorus of "Super Bass" by Nicki Minaj. And when I told her so, we both exploded with laughter. I'd forgotten how entertaining it was to have a ukulele-playing rock star check your heart palpitations.

"Let's do this every night," she declared.

With relief, I smiled a wholehearted yes. *It was not too late to seize the gift.*

Next, it was Natalie's turn. With her, I was a little nervous. What if she had gotten too old for this? What if the mere thought of her mom's head on her chest weirded her out? What if she said yes but it was just plain awkward? I decided not to listen to the voice of discouragement—because what if it *did* work out? What if The Heartbeat Check was just what she needed tonight?

After we read a chapter of her Nancy Drew mystery together, I swallowed the lump in my throat and took the direct approach. "Would you mind if I listen to your heartbeat like I used to?"

Natalie gave me an exasperated look as if to say, "Are you serious, Mom?" But I noticed she didn't say no. Her eyes slowly rolled upward as she considered my request. Finally, this child who adamantly chooses her own clothes, walks by herself to her friend's house, and wears deodorant four out of seven days a week informed me that it would be okay.

Then she did exactly what she had done when she was younger: she inhaled my scent and said, "Your hair smells so good, Mama."

While listening to the steady beat of her heart, I remembered that she liked me to interpret what I heard. "Your heart sounds sleepy tonight, Natalie. Perhaps it was all those laps you did at swim-team practice or the way you tackled that entire page of math problems after school."

"What else could it be, Mama?" she asked, interested in what other noteworthy things I had noticed about her that day. It was comforting to know that although my child had grown in height and years, she had not outgrown this special ritual. *It was not too late to seize the gift.* I promised myself that I'd try to keep it going for as long as my children would allow and have strived to uphold that vow. Although there are occasions when *The Heartbeat Check* is trumped by a late arrival home or an extensive homework assignment, nearly all our nightly tuck-ins conclude with the rhythmic sound of two growing human beings. While one girl's heartbeat check brings laughter so intense that hiccups result, the other child's heartbeat check inspires solemn talks of surgery, death, heaven, poverty, and pollution.

Yet, there is one commonality.

The Heartbeat Check offers refuge.

No matter how crazy the day … no matter how discouraged I feel … no matter how dismal the state of our nation, *The Heartbeat Check* offers sanctuary.

It brings clarity when I am conflicted …
It brings calm when I am in chaos …
It brings direction when I am lost …
It brings peace when I am overwhelmed …
It brings redemption when I've failed …
It brings inspiration when I feel unmotivated …

But that is only the half of it.

Sometimes I'll walk by Natalie's room as she's placing her head on the chest of Banjo the cat. "I'm doing a Purr Check," she explains with a smile. I have to hold back tears knowing this connective ritual is an even greater gift than I ever could've imagined: *The Heartbeat Check* is God's quiet retreat for those growing up in a world of distractions.

Perhaps one day when my children are adults and life just looks too bleak ... or the news is too disturbing to hear ... or the schedule is too packed ... or the distance between themselves and the people they love is too vast, they will remember where to find solace.

And when they draw their loved one close, they will be reminded that the sound of hope is merely a heartbeat away. It is never too late to lay aside past regrets or future worries and listen for it.

 ## HANDS FREE LIFE DAILY DECLARATION

Today I will set aside my insecurities and ask my spouse, child, parent, or loved one if I can hold them close. I will listen to their heartbeat, breathe in their scent, and tell them how much I love them. There will be obstacles and challenges that will interfere in carrying out these moments of connection, but I will not let the distractions of my life stop me from investing in what matters most—at least not today.

HANDS FREE LIFE HABIT BUILDER 1

Fill the Spaces of Life by Taking Off the Ticking Clock

I take off the ticking clock to sit on floor of my child's bedroom as she holds up every single shirt she owns, contemplating which one to wear to school the next day.

I take off the ticking clock to listen to my husband talk sports scores, politics, and grilling techniques.

I take off the ticking clock when my parents provide detailed medical commentary and exercise reports when asked how they are doing.

I take off the clock when my child shows me how she can do her own hair for school—a style that takes no less than seven minutes and resembles a bird's nest in the back when complete.

I take off the clock when my little nephew and I take a walk around the block and he wants to put every "wock" he finds in his pocket.

I take off the clock when I kneel beside my sleeping child and recite prayers of gratitude that morning chaos has a way of squelching.

These offerings of my time, presence, and patience often require deep breaths from me, a Reformed Rusher. But with every triumph over my former rushing ways, I heal a little more. I feel at peace knowing I am exactly where I need to be.

I know every minute of life cannot be lived like this. We have responsibilities, commitments, bills, deadlines, and duties. But when I take time to open my eyes, my heart, and my hands, I become aware that there is often something more pressing at hand.

There must be time to wave to the elderly man across the parking lot.

There must be time to ask the cashier how her day is going.

There must be time to kiss the man I love before we go our separate ways.

There must be time to notice the ladybugs that flitter across our path.
Because when I find myself thinking there isn't time to wait as worn-
out shoes shuffle across an intersection, to look into hopeless
eyes and offer a smile, or kiss the lips of the ones who saved me
from my distractions, I might as well strap that ticking clock back
around my neck and struggle for my next breath.
But I refuse to live my life by the sound of a ticking of a clock.
The sound of my own steady breath and the heartbeats of the people
I love are the sounds that make life worth living.

The next time you yearn to fill the spaces of your life and be all there,
try using the visual image of physically removing the heavy clock from
around your neck. Feel the weight being lifted off your chest as you give
yourself permission to be in one place and one place only. Remind yourself
these are the spaces where real living occurs and you have every right to
devote time and attention to the most important spaces of life.

Habit 2:

SURRENDER CONTROL

←———— ♥ ♥ ♥ ————→

Surrender to what is. Let go of what was. Have faith in what will be.

Sonia Ricotti

IT WAS THE WORST case of the stomach flu I'd ever experienced. After being awake the entire night, I managed to make my way to the living room couch, where I collapsed in agony.

With Scott away on a business trip and my family living several states away, there was no one to come to my rescue. Normally I would've worried about how Natalie and Avery, then ages eight and five, would be cared for. But the only thing on my mind was how I would survive the next wave of nausea.

Suddenly two bright, smiling faces with morning bedhead hovered over me. "Don't worry; we'll handle everything," the big one consoled.

Handle everything? They can't even pick up dirty underwear from their bedroom floor, I scoffed to myself, fearing how the next twenty-four hours would play out.

I closed my eyes, planning to rest for just a few minutes, but woke up hours later. Surrounding my lifeless body were teetering stacks of (nearly) folded laundry. Next to my head was a metal cookie sheet acting as a hospital tray. It held a large ice water with a straw and three Saltine crackers on a pristine white napkin.

The girls appeared before me both fully dressed. Natalie sported a ponytail and Avery had managed to comb the front of her hair. The back of her head resembled a mound of dryer lint, but I wasn't judging; I was wearing pillow marks on my face and two-day-old pajamas.

The kitchen timer began going off. Were they using the oven? I panicked.

"Don't worry, Mama. We made lemon-poppy-seed bread," Natalie assured me, as if two small children baking bread was a routine thing around here. "And we cleaned up our mess when we were finished," she added, as if reading my mind.

Thinking I was surely dreaming, I struggled to pull myself up to peer over the top of the couch. With an oven mitt on each hand, the girls were admiring a grossly misshapen loaf of bread as if they'd just produced a bar of gold.

Within minutes they congregated at the kitchen table with thick slices of steamy bread slathered in butter. Engaged in critical baking evaluation, they quickly forgot about their sickly mother balled up in the fetal position on the couch.

"It's not as sweet as the bread Mama makes, but I think it's better this way," said one.

"Yeah, definitely better. We should totally take over the baking in this house. What should we try next time?" said the other.

As I listened to them collaborate, problem solve, and dream up future baking pursuits, two fat tears slid down my cheeks. It had been a rough twenty-four hours, but that is not why I cried. I cried because right before my weary eyes, I saw my children reaching their potential. Although I had not been there to monitor that heaping teaspoon of baking soda or that extra ten minutes of baking time, things had turned out just fine—actually, better than fine. My children's faces held the unmistakable glow of ungoverned triumph.

The truth is, had I not been sick, I would have tried to control the situation. Because that is what I did. In my haste to get things done quickly with the least amount of mess ... in my effort to avoid conflict and achieve the best results ... in my quest to protect my children from harm and failure ... in my pursuit to appear as if my children and I had it all together, I attempted to control everything, including people, events, time, and situations. But seeing my children soar to heights unimagined during my illness enabled me to I see what I failed to see before. My need for control was holding us *all* back from fulfilling life experiences, meaningful connection, and transformational growth. By micromanaging our lives in small and big ways, I was missing the joy found in carefree living and lumpy loaves of bread made with love. I didn't want to miss any more. I vowed to begin releasing my grip — and not just in the kitchen.

While interacting with my parents, family, work associates, and children I taught at church, I made every effort to step back and let others take the lead. Because tasks did not have to be carried out *my* way, for once I found myself learning too. It was okay to be wrong or not know the answer. No longer did I feel pressured to be the expert or the taskmaster. Yes, there were more messes and mistakes, but there was also more laughter, more autonomy, and more joy from unplanned results. Making it my daily practice to surrender control over situations, people, and events led to the ultimate freedom: allowing my life to evolve according to God's plan rather than *my* plan.

Surrendering Control, the second intentional habit of a Hands Free Life, allows everything and everyone to simply *be*. Because you are no longer managing, predicting, or regulating people and situations, you have an expanded view. At last you are able to see opportunities to connect to what really matters in authentic, spontaneous ways. In this chapter, we'll explore how surrendering control frees us to live better and love more. It is my hope that you will be inspired to let life happen the way it's meant to happen — even when it feels uncomfortable, inconvenient, scary, or too late to even try. After all, how are we able to witness the beautiful results of allowing something to naturally unfold if we hold it captive to our plan? There is a much bigger plan than we could ever imagine for ourself, our family, and our life's work that can only be seen when we stand back and behold the beautifully lopsided results of life being lived.

SURRENDER CONTROL TO BE FREE OF PAST MISTAKES

It was my first time participating on a parenting panel. Mike Robbins and Michelle Gale, experts in the field of living with intention and gratitude, joined me at the front of the room. Having participated in this conference format many times before, Mike and Michelle were relaxed, assuring me the discussion was going to be great. As panel moderator, Mike decided he would pose questions based on the feel of the audience. "We'll just let things flow and see where it takes us," he said casually.

Panic gripped me. Letting things "flow" was not how I operated. There was always, *always* a plan—especially when it came to public speaking. I always had some idea of what I was going to say in response to every question. I'm pretty sure Mike could see the blood draining from my face. He gently touched my shoulder and assured me he would jump in if I got stuck.

I nervously took my seat next to Michelle and realized this would be the first time I was seated while speaking to an audience. Naturally my eyes were drawn to the people seated in the front row. I smiled. They smiled back. They are nice people, I repeated to myself several times. Even if I drew a blank or became tongue-tied, they didn't look like individuals who would laugh at me, I desperately hoped.

Mike began posing questions: *When did you realize you were living distracted? What was your first step to becoming more present?* I was so relieved! I knew those answers! I began sharing my journey with "my people" in the front row. It wasn't long before I forgot I was holding a microphone or talking to a large group of people.

It wasn't long before I forgot what I was "supposed" to be saying and just spoke from the heart. One man in a red sweater nodded encouragingly, just like a friend sitting across from me at a coffee shop. Another man clapped enthusiastically after one of my responses. One woman, whose thick, dark hair swooped over her left cheek, could not stop her tears. I was speaking to those people, literally and figuratively. I could feel it, and it made me want to openly share more.

About midway through the discussion, Mike invited the audience to participate in a group exercise. He instructed them to complete the following sentence with a partner:

If you really knew me, you would know . . .

After each person took a turn, he or she was instructed to go a little deeper:

If you really, really knew me, you would know . . .

The partners were encouraged to exchange their truths until time was up.

Although Mike had checked with Michelle and me ahead of time, I shifted uncomfortably in my chair when Mike said that the panelists would go first to illustrate the exercise.

Part of me hoped my microphone would malfunction or I would suddenly lose my voice. Part of me wanted to think of something light and easy that would make people laugh. Part of me wanted to get up and run away.

Because the truth was, I did not have a prepared response. I'd never been asked this question. Therefore, I would be forced to do something completely out of my element—just let things "flow."

I prayed for God's guidance and rested my eyes on my supporters in the front row. Their loving gazes indicated I would be safe and encouraged, no matter what I said.

And what came out of my mouth was not at all what I expected. I said:

"If you really knew me, you would know I have trouble forgiving myself for the mistakes of my past. You see, I missed a lot of important moments in my children's lives due to my distracted, perfectionistic, hurried ways. And when my readers write to me and say, 'I've made a lot of mistakes. Is it too late for me?' I tell them, 'It's never too late. Today is a new day. This journey is not about yesterday. It is about today and the critical choices you make today.' That is what I tell my readers. That is what I believe with all my heart. But yet, I cannot offer those same forgiving words to myself."

And then I took it one step further:

"If you really, really knew me, you would know that I've apologized to my daughters for the impatient, unhappy, perfectionistic drill sergeant I once was and for the hurt I caused ... but when they wrap their arms around my neck and say, 'I forgive you, Mama,' I can't quite allow myself to accept or embrace their forgiveness. For some reason, I keep revisiting past mistakes, as if to punish myself."

As I set down the microphone, I felt a single tear slide down my face. I'd never said those things to myself, much less an entire roomful of people, but for some reason I did not feel embarrassed or ashamed. In fact I felt lighter, as if a heavy burden had been lifted.

As audience members paired up and began doing the exercise, I watched their faces. I noticed the way people locked eyes. I saw some lean forward. I saw nodding heads and compassionate expressions. A deep connection between people who had never met was palpable. I vowed to remember what happened in that moment when we stopped controlling every word and allowed our innermost truths come to the surface. Barriers had crumbled, and the past lost a little of its oppressive grip with the empowerment that came with confession.

After the panel discussion, a young woman who'd volunteered at the conference for several years approached me. "The way you and your colleagues openly shared your hearts changed the atmosphere of the entire room and brought people together. Your willingness to be vulnerable touched lives here today, and it will affect the entire conference, maybe even the world," she said hopefully.

I was hopeful too. I wanted more than anything to remain on this course toward true freedom, but this conference room of supportive strangers had acted as a safe haven for me that day. Would I be able to keep letting go of past mistakes amidst the challenges and pressures of real life?

Two days later, I had my chance. I was lying next to Natalie at bedtime, and she was telling me about the discomfort she felt while I was at my conference. "I couldn't fall asleep when you were gone. I missed you tucking me in," she whispered in the sanctity of her darkened room. "It helps me calm down to talk to you," she added.

Your daughter needed you and you were not here, Guilt scolded, eager to add one more infraction to my long list of mistakes.

Remembering my vow from the conference, I shushed that harsh voice and focused on what my child was saying right here and now. "So finally I went downstairs and got a pair of your pajama pants and slept with them," Natalie continued. "When I could smell your smell, I felt better. It helped me sleep. Then I was okay."

In other words, my daughter spoke these words to my heart:

I don't care where you've been. I'm just glad you are here now.
I don't keep track of your failings. I'm just glad you are here now.
I don't remember your mistakes. I'm just glad you are here now.
Because you know what comforts me? You—not what you did do or didn't do last week, two month ago, or two years ago. You—the mere smell of your presence comforts me.

Sometimes God speaks to me in whispers; other times, he uses a bullhorn. Through Natalie's message, I was powerfully reminded of God's promise: "There is no distance too vast, no mistake too severe that could ever separate me from your love." And like my daughter clung to those pajamas pants while I was away, I am now resting in these hope-filled truths:

Let us not be so consumed with the past that we forget we are here now.

Let us not be so bent on self-protection that we never speak our innermost hurts.

Speaking one's deepest regrets does not change the past; it does something far greater. It connects us to the One who loves us despite our faults and failings so that we are free to connect to the person sitting beside us. This type of vulnerable connection, born of a place of deep pain and authenticity, is the kind of connection that is strong enough to transform individuals, families, communities, cities, and worlds.

Let us surrender the failures and pains of our past so that our love is not separated and weakened but instead united and strengthened.

 ## HANDS FREE LIFE DAILY DECLARATION

Today I will be at peace with who I once was and feel hopeful for the person I am becoming. I will not view the mistakes of yesterday as failures but instead as stepping stones to the lovingly imperfect, grace-filled life I've always wanted to live. Who I am becoming now is more important than who I was then.

SURRENDER CONTROL TO BROADEN FUTURE OPPORTUNITIES

Natalie was fifteen months old when I first felt the desire to "freeze" her in time. She walked to the kitchen to greet me, just like she did every morning. She shuffled along in pajamas with built-in feet—the only kind she wore despite the fact we lived in Florida. Her diaper (which we were hip enough to call "diap" for short) protruded in the back, tempting my hand to give it a loving pat.

Natalie had a ridiculous amount of jet-black hair that stood up in random directions, yet always had the right amount of "puff" when she awoke. My child was happy— such a happy little morning person that I couldn't help but be happy too. And although I was new to this mom gig, I had an unsettling feeling that *this* wouldn't last. She would change. And although my rational mind knew I would love the older version of my beautiful child just as much as this pocket-size one, my heart hurt knowing I would never see her just like this again.

I experienced the same desire to preserve her in time on the eve of her third Halloween. I wanted to freeze her as she twirled proudly in her Snow White costume ... when she danced to "Thriller" in our neighbor's driveway ... when she rolled on the floor laughing uncontrollably from too many Reese's Peanut Butter Cups. I kissed her chocolate-covered face and swore I never wanted her to outgrow that costume or my arms ... ever.

I also wanted to freeze her on the first day of kindergarten ... the way she bravely let go of my hand at the entrance of the school ... the way her big brown eyes looked directly in my eyes as she said, "I'll be okay, Mama" ... the way she turned and looked back only once before walking into the big, uncharted world without me.

Later, I wanted to freeze her at age seven when she was challenged to a race by older boys from the neighborhood. She flew past the boys on the playground, hair flying and fearlessness etched into her gorgeous face. Suddenly, the realization that she possessed the strength and determination to do anything she wanted in life was as clear as her feet were steady.

I have a "freeze" list for Avery too. It includes the time she sang "Amazing Grace" with the voice of an angel and included a glorious pause midperformance to savor an adult-size yawn. And that day at Siesta Key Beach when we were unexpectedly knocked over by a playful wave. I literally fought back the tears as she pursed her exquisite pink lips tightly together and then happily declared, "Salt water tastes an awful lot like wasabi."

Each time I felt this sense of longing to stop time and capture my child at that particular age, I let my desire be known. "Please don't grow," I'd beg my child with her cheek pressed up against mine. "Stay little forever, won't you?" I teased, thinking it was the greatest tribute to Father Time, who I too often failed to appreciate and too often wasted on things that didn't matter. What I failed to see was what such a request was doing to the ones who could not give me what I asked for. Thankfully, Avery enlightened me.

The subject came up during a one-on-one lunch date between Avery and my mother. In the midst of discussing her upcoming birthday, my child divulged this little bombshell: "My mom doesn't want me to grow."

Although my mother gently pointed out that her granddaughter was not traumatized when she spoke these words, nor was she upset, Avery had clearly said, "My mom doesn't want me to grow up, but I do want to grow up, Grandma. I do."

To say my heart stopped would be an understatement. As my mother relayed this illuminating conversation to me, my hand flew to my gaping mouth and my mind raced with the possible implications of my past actions. In my staunch belief that I was doing my children a favor by loving them so much I wanted to freeze them in time, I'd laid a mighty large burden on their shoulders.

Although Avery laughed every year when I jokingly said, "Please stay three" or "Let's just skip birthday number five," there was conflict in her heart. After all, children want to please their parents. Even at a young age, my child realized that out of anything in the world, she could not give me this. She did not have the ability to stop growing ... nor did she *want* to stop growing.

After concluding the conversation with my mom, I immediately went to Avery's room, where she was playing dolls. I sat down next to her on the floor, carefully tucking my legs behind my knees as I struggled to form the right words. I decided there was no point in beating around the bush. "I am so sorry I've been asking you to stay little. That is not fair of me to ask of you," I blurted out.

"Why?" Avery asked with a mixture of surprise and skepticism based on this sudden change of heart from her mother.

I admitted to her that although it was difficult to see her do more and more things without my help, I wouldn't want it any other way. I told her it was my daily blessing to watch her get taller, stronger, and more independent. I assured her that my love had no age limit. "I will love you when you are a sixteen-year-old teenager driving a car. I will love you on the day you say, 'I am ready to live on my own.' I will love you on the day you get your first gray hair!" I concluded with six powerful words: "I love to watch you grow."

Avery wrapped her arms around my neck and heaved an enormous sigh. I, on the other hand, fought back tears. Why was I having such an emotional reaction to this surrender with Father Time? I wondered. *She wants to grow. This is okay. In fact, this is the way it should be!* I reminded myself.

As if fate knew my newfound resolve needed to be put to the test, Natalie asked if she could start a daily exercise regime just like the one I had with my sister, Rebecca, when I was in grade school. Instantly, I regretted telling my children (whenever they whined about chores) that one of my summer duties as a child was to go for a walk each day with my sister.

Natalie laced up her shoes while waiting to find out if she could take her little sister around the small loop in our subdivision. I recited a new mantra: *My children want to grow. My children need to grow. I will let them grow.* I swallowed the lump in my throat and agreed to their independent adventure around the block. We discussed exactly where they would jog, and although no one seemed to care what I would be doing, I informed them that I would wait in the yard. The sisters ran off together without even looking back. I wiped my sweaty hands on my pants and assured myself it was time to do this. Then I waited.

Within four minutes, Avery came bounding around the corner. Despite the reddish hue from exertion, her face donned a glorious smile that accentuated her achievement. After describing

53

the details of her "jog," she reminded me that Natalie was going do the larger loop and would be back in a few minutes. So I waited some more.

After counting every mosquito bite on Avery's legs and investigating a massive anthill next to the mailbox, I began to wonder why Natalie had not returned. I watched nervously as a dark cloud edged closer to our vicinity. I alternated glances between the threatening cloud and the street corner, praying I would see a blonde ponytail flying in the wind before the sky opened up.

No such luck. It began to pour. I raced inside to get my car keys and assured my terrified-looking child that we would find her big sister.

As I was carefully inching my car from the garage, Natalie sprinted through the grass and found refuge on the porch. Unfortunately, I did not see her huddled against the door because I was already searching the street with frantic eyes.

Avery and I made the full loop and saw no sign of Natalie. In a panic, my mind began playing out every misfortune that could come to her. I imagined a pedophile in a van with tinted windows. I imagined a freak lightning strike coming out of nowhere. I imagined a distracted driver fumbling with her phone as rain-covered streets became slick. I imagined rabid dogs, amnesia, and potholes the size of small cars. "I've lost her!" I cried out. "It's my job to keep her safe, and I failed her," I sobbed irrationally as I gripped the wheel with white knuckles.

Between the rain coming down on the windshield and the tears streaming down my face, I just barely detected a dot of color on our front porch. It was Natalie in her blue shirt! I swerved into the driveway, my eyes already examining her from head to toe. Other than looking a little worried and a little wet, she appeared perfectly fine.

As Avery and I ran toward her, I could hear her explaining the rationale for her actions with adult-like maturity. "I saw you leave to go find me, so I knew it would be best to stay here and not try to run after you."

Avery reached the porch before I did, practically knocking Natalie over with on overly enthusiastic embrace. That's when the two began talking and I faded into the background.

"I was thinking I wouldn't have a sister anymore ... and that made me cry," whimpered the small one.

"It's okay. Everything's fine," assured the big one, gulping down any remaining hint of fear in her voice. "Besides, you did great today," Natalie cheered as she hugged her sister. "I watched you run all the way home. And then I made it all the way around—even in the rain! We'll do it again tomorrow. Next time we'll check the weather radar before we go, okay?" The girls smiled at each other in agreement.

Next time? The fear in me swelled. I didn't want there to be a next time. I didn't want anything bad to happen. I didn't want to let them get out of my sight ever again. But alas, I knew there would be a next time. I would let them take this walk again tomorrow. Eventually it would lead to more, longer adventures like sleep-away camp, job interviews on the opposite coast, and perhaps missions trips on the other side of the world. Yes, there would be a next time. Because holding my children captive in time and place meant depriving them of moments like this— moments when they learn to make smart decisions that will help them navigate the world without me.

Seeing them hold one another was one of the most meaningful sights I'd ever laid eyes on in all my years as a parent. But much to my surprise, I did not think to myself, "I want to freeze them." Instead I thought:

> I want to let go and watch my children grow
> and run
> and dream
> and create
> and console.
> I want to watch my children grow
> and fall down
> and get up

and help
and heal.
I want to watch my children grow,
with joy on my face,
gratitude in my heart,
and prayers of protection on my breath.

Although tears may still spring up as I realize with bittersweet emotion that another stage of my child's life has passed, I intend to open my hands to the blessing of growth. I will call it: *Letting go of my children in time* ... in *their* time. Prepare to see me on the sidelines, no caution tape in hand, watching in quiet joy as my children go forth, carrying my love and support on their small but sturdy shoulders.

 ## HANDS FREE LIFE DAILY DECLARATION

Today I will acknowledge that my life is not quite what I expected. My children/marriage/career/dream are not turning out exactly as planned, but that doesn't mean things are going wrong. In these diversions from the path I imagined, there are blessings seen and unseen. Today I will open myself up to greater possibilities by abandoning the way I think it should be and just let it be.

SURRENDER CONTROL TO FULFILL YOUR LIFE'S PURPOSE

I will never forget the first time Avery put on eyeglasses. My little kindergartener practically salivated in the vision center as the technician casually buffed the lenses before handing them over. Avery slid the pair of glittery pink rims on her face and peered in the mirror. BAM! My typically smiley girl, who all along was merely a bud, exploded into full bloom. As I marveled at this radiant child in spectacles, three words came to mind: *Sunflower on Steroids.*

While most people, adults and children alike, often flinch, cry, or curse at the first sight of themselves in obtrusive eyewear, my child delighted in it. As Avery brought the small mirror to her smiling face, tears sprang to my eyes and a sigh of relief escaped from my lungs. I was grateful that she liked her glasses but, more importantly, that she liked *herself* in them. It did not go unnoticed to my people-pleasing heart that my daughter did not turn to the technician, her big sister, or me to ask, "What do you think?" Avery loved those glasses and that was all she needed to know.

I fully expected her intense optical love to wane, but it never did. In fact, watching Avery put on her glasses became my favorite part of the day. Each morning I gently rubbed away the smudges while Avery stood there in eager anticipation of the beloved spectacles being placed on her face. Judging by her expression you would have thought I was about to squirt whipped cream directly into her mouth or hand her a certificate that said, "Actually, you *can* suck your thumb for the rest of your life."

It was hard to believe a pair of glasses could cause that explosion of happiness on Avery's face. There she stood, displaying utter and complete joy as she looked at life through those little rims. I was in awe ... and a tiny bit jealous. *What the heck does she see when she peers through those things?* I wondered to myself every single morning.

I really wanted to write about those eyeglasses, that expression, that confidence. I just knew there was something there, a huge Hands Free discovery just waiting to be revealed. So when I was asked to write a piece for a hugely popular parenting website, I was determined to write about the glasses. But after several days of blank pages and hair pulling, I gave up on the glasses. Instead I wrote about getting lost with three preschoolers when chaperoning a field trip and the Hands Free lessons that came with the experience. I took a risk and used humor along with my typical painful truths to describe my revelations. I couldn't wait to see the response.

On the day my story was published, I posted a short introduction for my blog readers that directed them to the post on the parenting site. Within a few minutes of the post hitting my subscribers' in-boxes, I received two emails notifying me of subscription cancellations. Two people had decided they no longer wanted to subscribe to "Hands Free Mama." Instantly I wondered what I had done "wrong." As feelings of rejection, shame, and insecurity washed over me, I mentally reviewed my post section by section to see if I could figure out where I had offended.

While I was busy scrutinizing my writing abilities and considering alternative careers, I failed to see the beauty before me. I failed to delight in the way I had come up with creative nicknames for each preschooler based on their personality. I failed to recall how my heart had soared when I figured out the perfect final sentence to conclude the story. I failed to rejoice in the lives touched—those who wrote, "I needed these words today." I failed to see that I was doing a job I loved—an occupation I'd dreamed of having since I was eight years old. All these beautiful details were mine for the taking, and I couldn't see them. I was fixated on the fact that I had failed to please everyone. I was too busy trying to control something I had no control over.

As those unsubscribe notifications glared at me from my computer in-box, a solution became immediately apparent. Being notified when a reader unsubscribed from my blog was not automatic; this was an optional setting. With newfound clarity, I decided I would no longer voluntarily subject myself to feelings of rejection and failure.

I logged into my subscription service and triumphantly unchecked the box that read, "Send me an email when people unsubscribe." Originally I thought this information would help me become a better writer, but there are much healthier ways to improve one's craft. The fact is, I will never know why someone decides he or she no longer wants to receive my posts. It may have something to do with what I wrote, and it may not. But even more importantly, *it doesn't matter.* I must continue to write because this is what makes my soul come alive. I must write because I believe this is my life's purpose. And knowing someone does not want to read my writing (for whatever reason) only causes me to second-guess my abilities and hinders me from living the life I am meant to live.

A few days after I unclicked the box on my subscription service, Avery and I were going through the morning lens-cleaning ritual. As usual, she was staring at her glasses in eager anticipation of their arrival to her face. I took a deep breath, knowing it was time—the lesson of the little glasses was about to impact me like the sight of a rainbow after a long, hard rain. Now I was ready.

"Why do you smile so big every time you put on your glasses?" I asked, my voice heavy with hope.

There was no hesitation from my curly-haired, freckle-faced love. "Because I can see. I can see all the beautiful things."

Yes! Oh, my sweet child, yes! It is really that simple, isn't it? There are so many beautiful things to see, but when we spend too much time fixating on what *other people* want us to see, we miss them all.

The lesson of the little glasses is a powerful one, but we must be ready—ready to surrender the desire to please everyone ... ready to surrender the hope of being liked and accepted by everyone ... ready to surrender the fear of making mistakes. We must be ready to release our words, our choices, our dreams into the atmosphere knowing we cannot control other people's reaction to them.

Now that I've surrendered, I feel different. I am holding my shoulders and head higher. My voice embodies a new confidence. And I'm smiling—smiling like a little girl when she puts on her pink spectacles—because I am no longer waiting for someone to tell me what is beautiful, what is good, and what is of value.

Now I can see for myself.

HANDS FREE LIFE DAILY DECLARATION

Today I will stop looking at images and newsfeeds that take my focus off what really matters. Today I will distance myself from people who cause me to question what I know is right for me. Today I will discard or destroy items that open wounds from a dream never realized or a past hurt. Today I will offer myself a clear, unfiltered view of the beautiful life I am meant to live.

HANDS FREE LIFE HABIT BUILDER 2

Surrender Control by Opening Clenched Fists

Before, I was living life with critical hands,
Always demanding perfection.
Gotta be just right ... be just right.
Before, I was living life with tireless hands,
Always trying to please.
Gotta make everyone happy ... make everyone happy.
Before, I was living life with fretting hands,
Always asking, "What if?"
Gotta go according to plan ... according to plan.
Before, I was living life with full hands,
Always taking control.
Gotta do it myself ... do it myself.
But as I struggled to catch my breath day after day, I realized I was
    not living life, I was managing life. Because living life with a death
    grip is not living at all.
Deep in my soul, I yearned to grasp what really mattered,

And I knew I couldn't do it with clenched fists.
So I opened them with the word *surrender*.
When anxiety, fear, and controlling thoughts came into my head,
I physically opened my hands and whispered these words:
I surrender the pressure. I am doing the best I can.
I surrender my fear. There is a hedge of protection around my family.
I surrender my hate talk. My body can do remarkable things.
*I surrender my insecurities. What others think of me is not my
     business.*
I surrender my timetable. God's timing is perfect.
I surrender my blank page. Words will come when they are ready.
*I surrender my uncertainty. A resolution will come without my
     interference.*
With each surrender, I got a taste of true freedom.
With each surrender, I felt life coming back to my bones.
With each surrender, I saw positives in people and situations that I
     could not see before.
At last, with unclenched fists, love and life found their way back into
     my mind, heart, body, spirit, and soul.

Take a moment to think about the situations, fears, or events that cause you to feel controlling. Think of a phrase you can say to yourself when controlling thoughts threaten to take away opportunities to live freely and love fully. You might just discover that by surrendering your best-laid plans, an even greater plan has a chance to evolve—one that allows room for connection, laughter, love, growth, and grace.

Habit 3:

BUILD A FOUNDATION

←———— ❤ ❤ ❤ ————→

Imagine you felt accepted and supported just as you are, appreciated for everything you do, celebrated and observed in each new accomplishment and allowed time to explore, try, experiment and experience life without judgment or fear of failure. How would it feel to build a lifetime from this strong foundation?

Linda Hinrichs

GROWING UP, I ASSOCIATED the word *tornado* with the twister in *The Wizard of Oz*. Only a handful of times did my parents wake me up to seek shelter during a storm. Since nothing ever transpired during any of those severe weather events, the word *tornado* remained elusive throughout much of my life. I didn't fully understand what a tornado could do until I lived in Alabama for six years.

The morning after an F2 tornado came frighteningly close to our home, my daughters and I wandered the neighborhood to check on friends and assess the damage. Uprooted trees, gaping holes in roofs, and entire chimneys sitting on manicured lawns shook us to the core. We would soon learn that this damage was minimal compared to what neighboring counties would

HANDS FREE LIFE

experience a few hours later. That evening, a mile-wide tornado descended on homes, farms, and businesses, picking them up and spitting them out with no regard for life and loss.

Once emergency vehicles cleared the roadways in Tuscaloosa, the pastor of our church asked Scott if he would be trained as a leader of an UMCOR Early Response Team. Having a personal connection to some of the impacted families through his job, Scott eagerly accepted. His team would be assisting tornado survivors in removing trees and debris at the location of their home, or in some cases, where their home used to be.

The first day Scott went into the field seemed to drag on forever. Although the girls and I spent the day collecting supplies for those in need of food, water, clothing, and hygiene items, my mind was focused solely on Scott. I had a deep yearning to see and hear what my husband was seeing and hearing.

When Scott finally came home, his pace was slow and stiff. His clothes were covered in a layer of dust and grime. His shoulders sagged from exhaustion and devastation. I expected these things. What I didn't expect was the look in his eyes. The man standing before me was not the same man who had walked out of our house that morning.

"Tell me everything," I pleaded, knowing that I needed to learn from Scott's experience as much as he needed to process what he had seen. My husband didn't take off his steel-toe boots or remove the sweat-soaked hat from his head. He simply collapsed onto the worn seat cushion of our kitchen chair. I slid in next to him, my hands folded and fidgety in great anticipation of his words.

"I met Mr. Frank today," Scott began so ordinarily. "Frank and his wife, Betty, live on a meandering country road that once held five long-standing homes. The homes are now gone. My team was there to sift through the wreckage to find valuable family mementos. We weren't there five minutes when Frank pulled me aside and said he had everything that mattered."

"So his family was all safe?" I asked, trying to interpret what Scott meant.

64

"Well, that's the thing. Betty and Frank's beloved dog, Shelby, had been carried away by the tornado. Frank said he kept getting down on his knees, praying for his dog's return. He knew Shelby might not be alive, but he just wanted to have her back, no matter what condition." Scott removed his hat. With one hand, he squeezed the rim back and forth in rhythmic succession. "A few hours after praying about Shelby's whereabouts, Frank spotted a little black dot on top of the hill where his neighbor's house used to be. It was Shelby. Seeing the state she was in, Frank surmised the tornado had carried her for several miles. But when Shelby saw Frank, she ran. Broken and scared, Shelby ran down the hill into her master's arms."

I cupped my hand over my mouth to stifle an emotional outburst that had the potential to wake our sleeping children. That's when Scott's hand reached for mine. I noticed it was stained and blistered. "Frank lost everything, yet he was the most contented man I've ever met."

Scott and I sat in silence at the kitchen table as I digested this miraculous fact: *a mile-wide tornado ravished a man's home, yet his foundation was unshaken.* Mr. Frank would overcome. He would endure. He would even thrive, despite the challenges ahead. To me, this was the epitome of living Hands Free. To lose so much—your house, your possessions, your wealth, your security—and yet still have an unwavering sense of peace and fulfillment inside your heart. Because Frank carried his foundation on the inside, not the outside, he had solid footing that enabled him to hold on and carry on even in times of tragedy.

I was familiar with such a foundation. It was given to me at age sixteen. I was sitting on my green gingham comforter doodling in my spiral notebook when my mom came into my bedroom. I shot her a look of annoyance, as if she were interrupting a dictation to the Queen of England. Despite the fact that I was a selfish, cantankerous teen, I was not too self-absorbed to realize the words coming from my mother's mouth were not to be taken lightly. The grave inflection in her voice caused me to look up from the blue lines on my notebook paper. "Rachel," my mom said, holding a limp dishrag in her hands, "I want you to know that no matter what you do, your dad and I will always love you. No matter what happens, you can always come home."

In response, I nodded coolly and said, "Okay," like it was no big deal—but I knew it was a big deal. In the breath of two mere sentences, I became fully aware of just how much my parents love me and just how much God loves me. My fear of making mistakes too huge to forgive, my worry of not measuring up, my apprehension about taking risks or just being myself were put to rest. Standing on the unshakable foundation of unconditional love, I had an inner armor that could not be taken away. My parents kept their word throughout my years of foolish mistakes and repeated disappointments. When I published my darkest truths for the whole world to read, I knew the first people to be standing there with open arms would be my parents, just like Mr. Frank scooped up Shelby, battered and bruised, to carry her home.

Building a foundation, the third intentional habit of a Hands Free Life, is the fertile soil in which an individual's passion and purpose can freely flourish. Through daily rituals of presence, communication, and faith, we have the power to stay connected to what matters in a culture that often leads us astray. In this chapter, we'll consider three ways to build foundations that are unwavering despite worldly pressures and challenges. It is my hope that you will consider the impact of the following notion on your life or the life of someone you love: no matter how tattered and torn you are, no matter how many wrong turns you take, no matter how far off the beaten path you go, you will never be irretrievably lost.

Frank could not protect Shelby from the deadly twister that swept her away. My parents could not shield me from the painful mistakes and difficult situations I encountered throughout my life. Yet in both instances, there was someone waiting on the other side of that struggle. Enduring foundations built on presence and faith give us the freedom to live and love fully by providing a path that always leads home.

BUILD A FOUNDATION THROUGH LISTENING

Avery and I were the first ones to arrive home after an evening
swim meet. I sat in the driveway, staring at the closed garage door.
I didn't want to go inside.

"What are you waiting for, Mama?" Avery piped up from the
backseat.

"Nothing," I said quietly, forcing my hand to push the button
that would allow entry. I couldn't explain the dread I felt in my
stomach to anyone, especially to this child who loved her grandpa
more than life itself. The truth was, I feared what I was going to
find when I went into the house. My dad, who was visiting from
Florida, had fallen ill that afternoon and had not been able to go to
the swim meet. Although he'd promised not to descend the stairs
while we were gone, I hadn't been able to help but worry about
my seventy-four-year-old diabetic father throughout the entire
swimming competition.

As Avery and I climbed the stairs, the feeling of angst I felt
at the meet was now going into overdrive. I'd hoped to find my
dad sleeping soundly, but the guest bed was empty. My perceptive
child knew this was not a good sign. "Uh-oh. Where's Paw Paw?"
she asked with wide eyes and worry in her voice.

I swallowed hard. "Oh, I'm sure he's around here somewhere."
My voice was steady and lighthearted even though the panic in
my chest was now nearly suffocating. "Why don't you go to your
bedroom and put on your pajamas while I look for Paw Paw," I
suggested, not knowing what condition I might find my father in.

After putting up a brief protest about wanting to help find
her lost grandpa, my child obliged. As soon as she reached her
bedroom, I bolted down the stairs. I immediately noticed the
front door was unlocked, which was not how we'd left it. I envisioned my pajama-clad father wandering the neighborhood in a
disoriented state or lying facedown in the grass.

Quickly scanning the street and yard, I saw no sign of him.
Now more worried than ever, I fought the urge to scream my
dad's name like a maniac. Instead I returned to the house and

searched every room. When I'd run out of places to look, my eyes began to water. I knew this was no time to cry or fall apart, so I willed myself to stay calm and think rationally. That's when it hit me. My dad's favorite place to sit was the back porch! Even on the hottest afternoons in the South, my dad would sit there content-edly gazing at the swaying trees or catching a catnap.

I rushed to the backdoor and immediately felt fear's intense grip release my racing heart. There sat my dad, hands folded and head bowed in peaceful slumber. My hand hastily reached for the doorknob, but I didn't turn it. I just stood there for a moment reciting a prayer of gratitude to God—thankful for one more day with my dad.

As tears of relief spilled from my eyes, words written by my dad came back to me in full force. I'd received an email message from him a few months into my Hands Free journey. While tell-ing me he was proud of my decision to transform my distracted ways to be fully present in my life, my father had his own difficult truths to share.

"I am sorry I was distracted while raising you and your sister," Dad wrote. "I wasn't as Hands Free as I could have been. I am deeply sorry for that. Growing up, I hope you always knew how much I love you." Dad didn't go into detail about what he was sorry for—he didn't need to. I knew. I remember. But I remem-ber something more—something much more important than my father's failings.

I remember walking across campus to my dad's office every day after school for over a decade. Upon my arrival, I would find my dad sitting at his desk surrounded by piles of papers and books. Although the empty chair sitting beside him was probably for a colleague in need of curriculum guidance or a college student seeking scheduling assistance, I always believed that empty chair was for me.

Dad would look up from whatever he was doing and greet me with a smile. Then, as if on cue, he'd place the cap on the black felt-tip pen he always used to grade papers or draft lecture notes.

The pen cap gesture was my signal. It meant my dad wanted to hear about my day. Sometimes I told him just a few things; other times I went on and on about something exciting or unusual that happened at school. My dad would listen, nod, and sometimes add his two cents. Without fail, my dad would smile as if hearing about *my day* was the best part of *his day*.

From first grade through my senior year in high school, I had after-school chats with my dad at his office. I can't recall a time when he said he couldn't talk—even when he was writing his dissertation, dealing with difficult faculty issues, or facing university budget cuts. When I spoke, my dad was there—all there.

My dad wasn't perfect. He lost his temper sometimes. He worked too much. He experienced periods of depression. But even through the rough patches, my dad always listened to me. My dad was never too busy, too distracted, or too desolate to listen to what I had to say, even in the rough patches. So despite what the critics say—that giving a child our undivided attention creates a child who thinks the world revolves around him or her—I believe otherwise. *Having a parent who listens creates a child who believes he or she has a voice that matters in this world.*

> When you believe your voice matters, you have the strength to say, "Let me out of the car" when you feel you are in a dangerous situation.
>
> When you believe your voice matters, you have the courage to say *no* to harmful substances that can affect your ability to make decisions and prematurely end your life.
>
> When you believe your voice matters, you have the bravery to admit you made a mistake and use that experience to learn, grow, and do better next time.
>
> When you believe your voice matters, you have the confidence to reveal your most difficult truths so someone else doesn't feel alone in his or her struggles.

During these actual events in my life I could have suffered in silence, but instead I spoke up. Why? Because my dad listened to me as I grew. And what this means is there is hope, great hope, for those who yearn to build a solid foundation in the lives of the people they love. You see, perfection is not required in order to give someone a solid foundation. After all, there will be days when you are dealing with heavy, soul-crushing issues. There will be days when nothing you do feels like enough. There will be days when smiles don't come easily and harsh words are spoken too quickly. On those days, I urge you not to say things like, "I'm a failure" or "I'm a bad parent" or "Nobody needs me." Instead, I urge you to garner the strength, the patience, the resolve to do one thing: *Listen.*

> Listen when she wants to tell you the (many) reasons she chose the pink shoes instead of the red ones. Listen when he tells you (in agonizing detail) how he built his giant Lego skyscraper.
> Listen when she tells you (for the fiftieth time) about the moment she met your father. Listen when he (annoyingly) chuckles his way through the time he drove his great-grandpa's tractor into the lake.
> Listen when he confesses he is struggling to make ends meet. Listen when she admits she hates how she looks.
> Listen when she reveals her fear of being alone. Listen when he admits you are his only hope.
> Listen with your eyes, ears, and heart. They know. They know when you are listening, and it matters; it really matters.

Because someday your loved ones will find themselves in a difficult situation, and they'll have a choice — either to suffer in silence or speak up. Perhaps that is the moment they will remember your eyes, the nodding of your head, your focus, your thoughtful response. Suddenly, they will be reminded that their voice holds value. Whether it's a plea, a confession, a protest, a blessing, or a prayer, your loved ones will find the strength to lift their voices. Perhaps they won't even know where that strength is coming from, but perhaps they will. All your mistakes that you thought were so unforgettable will be insignificant compared to the way you loved them by listening.

 ## HANDS FREE LIFE DAILY DECLARATION

Although I may fall short and make mistakes today, I can do one thing well: I can listen. I can look up when she walks in the room. I can focus on the color of his eyes when he speaks. I can look into his eyes before he gets out of the car. I can listen in a nonjudgmental and supportive way by nodding and smiling. I may not have all the answers, but I can listen. Because when it comes to building up a human being, unconditional attention is just as important as unconditional love.

BUILD A FOUNDATION THROUGH LIFELINES

I grew up equating handwritten notes with expressions of love. My mom worked long hours, so she often left small, square papers on the bed for my sister and me to find. Sometimes it was just a smiley face; other times she simply wrote the words *Love you!* in ordinary ballpoint pen, but it was more than enough. The way she didn't quite close the circle on the happy face and the way the letter *L* had a fancy loop were as comforting as the words that she wrote.

Lifelines—

Starting in elementary school, my mom requested I write notes to my grandma who lived a few hours away. What I loved the most is that Grandma always wrote back. The excitement I felt when I looked in the mailbox and saw a letter in my grandma's shaky font never disappeared. Even in college when there were tests to study for and social gatherings to attend, I took time to sit on my narrow bed and read my grandma's letters the moment they arrived. By studying her handwriting, I could tell how she'd been feeling that day. Toward the end of her time on earth, her script became barely legible. Those notes are now treasures connecting me to hugs that smelled of Kleenex, rose-scented lotion, and butterscotch candy.

Lifelines—

I'll never forget when the guy I was dating my senior year in college had a family emergency and had to take a sudden trip home. Sometime during the night, he'd dropped off a handwritten note telling me why he had to leave. A personal note of this nature from this particular guy seemed like a really big deal, and I felt incredibly excited by it. I tucked that note away for safekeeping, not knowing that message would be the first of many special letters from my future husband, Scott.

Lifelines—

The words *I'm proud of you* from my dad written in his signature black felt-tip pen, birthday notes from friends containing funny memories, and cards from my former students written in sublime kid penmanship are filed in a drawer next to my bed. Anytime I want to remember where I've been, what I am made of, or how immensely I am loved, I simply open that file. These touchable lifelines have played an important role in building the strong foundation on which I've navigated life. But it wasn't until I embarked on my Hands Free journey that I discovered lifelines could also be lifesaving.

Around the time I woke up to the fact that I was missing my life, Avery was learning to write words. As I took small steps to be more present in her life, she began writing me love notes. Although I'm sure the timing was purely coincidental, these tangible messages would come to me at the precise moment I needed to slow down and notice the blessings in front of my face. Avery's backward letters and childlike scrawl had a way of grounding me. I knew this beloved calligraphy was only temporary.

One morning I wrote, "I love you, Avery," on a yellow sticky note and placed it in Avery's lunch box, not realizing there was a blank one attached to it. When I cleaned out her lunch box that night, my love note had multiplied. I cried when I saw she'd written the same thing as me except she put my name where hers had been. Although her note to me said, "I love you, Mom," it might as well have said, "This is worth living for."

I reached up and, as a source of daily encouragement, stuck my daughter's note on the kitchen cabinet where the sandwich bread was stored. I taped another one of her notes in the pantry where the cereal was kept, then another in my clothes closet where I got dressed, and another on the bathroom mirror where I brushed my teeth. Wherever I turned, there was a Hands Free "stop sign" bringing my hurried, distracted, perfectionistic, and tech-obsessed self to a halt.

Although it came to the point that I no longer needed to post Avery's notes as visual reminders to pause for life and love, I knew I had experienced their lifesaving power for a reason. I anticipated the day when I'd write a lifeline that could potentially save someone else. I never expected it to be Natalie.

I took pen to paper when a beautiful and vibrant teen named Rebecca took her life after being a victim of cyberbullying. As I read the significant actions that Rebecca's mother, Tricia Norman, had taken to protect her daughter and remove her from the toxic environment, I couldn't help but weep knowing the tragic outcome. The mother noted that she'd thought things were going better for Rebecca at her new school, but the child had kept her distress from her family. "Maybe she thought she could handle it on her own," the mother was quoted as saying.[*]

Maybe she thought she could handle it on her own. I felt as if these ten words were a gift to me and to anyone listening. Natalie's exposure to the pressures and pain that came with growing up in a tech-saturated world were just beginning. I knew it was time to give Natalie tangible proof that she didn't have to go it alone. I consider the message I wrote to Natalie to be a lifeline for

* Lizette Alvarez, "Girl's Suicide Points to Rise in Apps Used by Cyberbullies," *NewYorkTimes.com* (September 13, 2013) http://www.nytimes.com/2013/09/14/us/suicide-of-girl-after-bullying-raises-worries-on-web-sites.html?pagewanted=all&_r=0.

anyone living in the twenty-first century ... a time when lives and reputations can be shattered with the click of a button ... where embarrassing mistakes are not limited to those who witnessed it but to thousands scrolling the social-media newsfeed ... where acceptance is based on appearance and status ... where public persona matters more than inner beauty, compassion, and kindness.

A TWENTY-FIRST-CENTURY LIFELINE TO MY DEAR NATALIE

Technology has become an integral part of your life now that you need it to complete your schoolwork. Eventually, you will want a phone and will want to start communicating with others online. Before that day comes, it is very important for me to tell you a few things. You will hear these words a lot from me—you might even get sick of them. But these reminders are important. When the time comes, you will know how important they are.

My reminders to you ...

TOMORROW HOLDS PROMISE

When you have been teased, hurt, or humiliated, that day will seem horrible and unbearable. Just know that when you make it through the day, tomorrow will bring a new light. Tomorrow holds possibilities that you cannot see today. I will help you see the promises in tomorrow when you can't.

MY LOVE FOR YOU CANNOT BE CHANGED

With me, you don't have to be strong. You can cry, scream, and let out your true feelings. My love for you cannot be changed by revealing the feelings going on inside you—no matter how hard they are to say out loud.

YOU ARE WORTHY OF LOVE

You are worthy of love and respect and kindness. If people hurt you, together we'll figure out a way to help you work through those problems, move on, or distance yourself from them if needed.

I encourage you to find that one loyal and kind friend with whom you can go through the school year. Don't let societal standards fool you into believing this friend must be popular, good looking, or cool; at the end of the day, kindness is the most important quality to have in a friend and be in a friend.

YOU POSSESS COURAGE AND STRENGTH

If you have been humiliated or teased, facing certain people may seem impossible. But you have the courage and strength within you to show others they cannot hold you back from living your life.

IT'S ABOUT THEM, NOT YOU

No matter how personal the attack, it is about them — their insecurities and their issues — not about you.

NO ONE CAN CHANGE THE WAY I SEE YOU

No matter how humiliated you are and no matter how embarrassing it is to tell me what happened, when I look at you, I see my beautiful and amazing child. No one can change the way I see you.

NOTHING IS TOO BAD TO TELL ME

You can come to me with anything — even if you made a mistake, even if you used bad judgment. There is nothing that is "too bad" to tell me. Believe me, I have made plenty of mistakes and even though it was hard to let someone else in, I was so relieved not to carry the burden alone.

LET AN ADULT KNOW

If your gut tells you what someone is doing is wrong, it probably is. Don't take part. Letting an adult know about someone who is being harmed or disrespected does not make you a coward — it makes you courageous and compassionate; it makes you a good friend who can look back on this later in life and proudly say, "I didn't turn the other cheek. I tried to help."

I cannot make your problems and hurts go away, but I can listen. And together we can come up with a solution. There is nothing we can't get through together. You are never, never alone.

I love you forever and always.

Mom

When I presented the note to Natalie at bedtime, I wasn't expecting her to pin it to her bulletin board amongst her other keepsakes. I wasn't expecting her to crawl into bed and ask if we could talk more about this. It quickly became apparent that she'd been waiting for an opening. Twisting the corner of her yellow bedsheet around her pointer finger, my daughter shared her own personal observations and experiences about peer alienation and ridicule. She maturely described how it felt to be betrayed by someone she trusted. That is when I told her about Rebecca and other young people who ended their lives as a result of being tormented.

Natalie sat up abruptly, as if the words she was about to speak could not be said lying down. "I would never kill myself, Mama! I have you, Daddy, Avery, and Banjo. I have too much to live for!" she said with conviction.

Not too long ago, I couldn't have imagined such grave words coming from my daughter's lips. Not too long ago, such words would have made me want to cry. But things are different now. Like so many others, the world of technology is pushing me into territories unknown, to places I never wanted to go. It is not possible to physically be by my loved one's side each time she enters dark territories of isolation and pain, but I can give her something to hold on to. I will fill the walls of her room and the walls of her heart with lifelines — tangible proof of where she's been, what she's made of, and how immensely she is loved.

HANDS FREE LIFE DAILY DECLARATION

What calms my child's school-day fears can be found in the smiley face above the letter *i*. What creates affirmation in the heart of my spouse can be posted on the bathroom mirror. What makes my friend feel beautiful can be written with a broad-tipped Sharpie and tucked beneath the windshield wiper of her car. What I believed in and how I loved can be evidenced in my handwriting long after I am gone. Today I will not assume they know how I feel. Today I will tell them by throwing out a lifeline. What really matters in life is literally at my fingertips.

BUILD A FOUNDATION THROUGH FAITH

Shortly after our family made an out-of-state move one summer, Avery began expressing worry about fitting in, new school routines, and homesickness. I took time to listen, assure, and empathize, but I knew it was time to lead her to something more comforting than any words I could give. I invited Avery to join me on my daily walk. Ever since my mom instilled the walking routine in me during grade school, I have literally walked my troubles away. Whether as a high school student, a young new teacher, a pregnant mother, or a full-time author, I have walked myself toward peace and clarity. I hoped that walking could help calm Avery's anxieties too.

I told Avery I'd discovered a beautiful tree-covered area not too far from our neighborhood. I warned her that we would first have to walk on a very busy road past a cemetery. Surprisingly, Avery had no interest in the shaded area but was captivated by the graveyard. It quickly became our routine to walk around looking at each stone and then resting on a wooden bench.

One morning we'd gotten there especially early. Dew still covered the ground. Avery noticed some new flowers propped up against a marble slab. "Do you think someone came here last night?"

"It sure looks like it," I said. "People come and visit the graves of their loved ones on the anniversaries of their death or their birthdays. Sometimes they come when they are worried about something and need someone to talk to. Sometimes they come to find comfort here, pray, or feel less alone."

"But there's no one here," she said, looking around just to make sure.

"Some of the greatest comforts in life come from things we cannot see, Avery. It's called faith," I offered.

"Oh," she responded, but I could tell that she needed more explanation to fully understand.

"Do you remember when Daddy was trained to help the people in Tuscaloosa dig out their most valuable possessions when the tornado destroyed their homes?" After Avery nodded, I continued. "Well, Daddy always had to ask the homeowner permission before he and his team removed any debris. This question revealed what was most important to people. I will never forget the stories of Miss Dottie and Mr. Franklin. Maybe hearing these stories will help you understand the meaning of faith."

Avery scooted closer, as if planning to stay awhile. I began describing two people I would never forget. Miss Dottie was a retired elementary-school teacher in her seventies. Her husband, a former professor, became very ill in the last years of his life. She cared for him in the corner bedroom of their ranch-style home before he passed away. Miss Dottie only wanted one thing from Scott and his relief team. She wanted to salvage the furniture from the room in which her dying husband had lived his last days. That is all she wanted. After removing the two-hundred-year-old fallen tree that had crushed that particular part of her home, the team relocated her husband's bed and chair to an undamaged section of her home.

Although I don't know this for sure, I envisioned what Miss Dottie did after the relief team left that day. I imagined she placed her fragile, aging body on her husband's bed. I imagined she stretched her body out but kept her arms wrapped tightly around her body. I imagined warm tears flowed down the sides of her face into her hair and onto the bed that had held her dear one. And for the first time since that tornado ripped through her house, I imagined Miss Dottie felt comfort. She couldn't see her husband, but he was there. He was there. She was not alone.

Mr. Franklin was in his sixties. He had been forced to retire from his occupation as a garbage collector when he fell from a garbage truck going thirty miles per hour. Mr. Franklin's knees were in bad shape, but that did not stop him from doing what he loved: gardening. When Scott asked the man how they could help in his recovery efforts, Mr. Franklin showed them his beautiful flowerbeds and lush garden that were now covered in disarray and destruction. Mr. Franklin only wanted one thing. He wanted to be able to access his garden. That is all he wanted.

As I did with Miss Dottie, I imagined what Mr. Franklin did after Scott's team prayed with him and went to their next work order. I imagined Mr. Franklin gingerly kneeling down in the rich, resilient Alabama soil. I imagined him digging his hands deep into the healing earth that quickly became saturated with his tears. And for the first time since the tornado shook the walls of his house, I imagined he felt comfort. He couldn't see God, but he knew God was there. God was there. Mr. Franklin was not alone.

After concluding the stories, I looked into Avery's face. "Those are stories of faith, Avery. Faith is a feeling deep inside you that God is working in your life even though you cannot see him. It is an unexplainable feeling of comfort that you are not facing life's challenges alone. And the reason I began taking you on walks is because when I walk, I feel like Miss Dottie lying on her husband's bed or Mr. Franklin digging in his garden. When I walk, I pray about my worries and my struggles. With each step I take, I become more and more comforted that things are going to be okay. The beautiful thing about faith is that it is in here," I said, touching her heart. "No storm, no out-of-state move, no human being can ever take it away. Someday you'll figure out what special activity brings you this unbreakable feeling of comfort."

"I already know, Mama," she said to my surprise. "When I sing, I feel safe. I feel warm." She stood up and walked around the gravestone. Now she had a story for me. "'Member when you asked me to bring my ukulele to Miss Angie's house after the tornado took her daughter away?" I nodded. "When I was singing 'Amazing Grace,' Miss Angie closed her eyes. I felt like she didn't want me to stop. I felt like my singing made her feel better. The whole room felt warm and safe."

The most comforting things in life cannot be seen, but they are felt. Avery had known this all along. And now she had just successfully described the only thing better than having faith; it is the moment your faith intersects with someone else's faith. Two people having faith together makes even the most challenging obstacle feel surmountable.

For the rest of the summer, Avery and I took a daily walk to the graveyard. I wasn't surprised when she began quietly singing to herself as the rush of morning traffic went by.

"What are you singing?" I asked one day.

"It's the song in my heart," she said. "Can you hear it?"

Despite the steady stream of cars and trucks, I could hear it. But even more, I could feel it: warmth, safety, and guidance. Because when you walk by faith, what you need to hear is felt above the noise and chaos of life.

HANDS FREE LIFE DAILY DECLARATION

Today I will resist the urge to get "one more thing" accomplished—instead I will engage in one activity that brings me peace and renewal. Today I will not seek fulfillment in material items that add more junk, more stress, and more worries to my life—instead I will find contentment in experiences of connection and thoughts of gratitude. Today I will act on the callings of my heart and not feel guilty about it. Today I will put what matters most—faith, family, friendship—at the top of the priority list.

HANDS FREE LIFE HABIT BUILDER 3

Build a Foundation with the Best Ten Minutes

Within my day, there will be time for the Best Ten Minutes:

Ten minutes to accept the most important invitations: yes to walking along the edge of the curb, yes to one more bedtime story, yes to face-to-face conversation …

Ten minutes to engage in activities that will better my life or the life of someone else, like creating art, making music, or building up another human being …

Ten minutes to learn something new about the people who share my life, ten minutes to learn something old in the pages of my grandmother's Bible …

Ten minutes to give the best kind of love—undistracted love.

Ten minutes to take the best kind of leap—the leap of faith.

Ten minutes to tuck a lifeline into a suitcase, a lunch box, or the pocket of worn blue jeans.

Ten minutes to lift a shaky voice toward heaven or wear down rubber treads walking toward clarity.

The Best Ten Minutes of each day are the building blocks of a solid
    foundation.
Through these life-giving investments, we are connected to what
    strengthens us, guides us, and fulfills us.
What is built in the Best Ten Minutes cannot be swept away in a
    storm, forgotten in a hotel room, divided in a divorce, or missed
    after a move.
Soon the Best Ten Minutes will become the most important minutes
    of the day.
Watch them as they grow from minutes to hours to days to years,
    eventually becoming a life worth living.

Ten minutes. That is where I started building a foundation based on the lasting and the permanent rather than the fleeting and the temporary. I locked my phone in a drawer, shut down my computer, pushed aside my to-do list, the guilt, and the regret to go to my child and hold her. She picked up my hand and kissed my palm. Her response motivated me to continue to make myself fully available for ten minutes each day to renew my spirit, my relationships, and my life's purpose. Those minutes grew and so did my foundation. Believe one small step can make a difference. Begin with the Best Ten Minutes.

PART TWO:

Living for Today

TAKE THE PRESSURE OFF

◄——— ⌄ ⌄ ⌄ ———►

You are your own worst enemy. If you can learn to stop expecting impossible perfection, in yourself and others, you may find the happiness that has always eluded you.

Lisa Kleypas

IT WAS SUPPOSED TO be a quick stop at a local hair salon to grab a styling product. But as I scanned columns and rows of creams and gels promising to make curly hair straight and straight hair curly, my attention was diverted. Seated in an oversize swivel chair was a freckle-faced young woman with distress in her eyes. On her lap were three bridal magazines splayed open—the weight of so many pages and so many choices threatening to cut off blood circulation to her legs. As one stylist busily adjusted a bridal hairpiece and another asked questions about its placement, I just couldn't avert my eyes. Uncertainty gripped the bride's youthful face as she contemplated her choices. I recognized that pained expression, the one that screamed, "It's got to be perfect!"

With a slight twist of her hand, the stylist spun the chair around. All I could see now was the back of the young woman's head. Her gorgeous waves of strawberry-blonde hair were tightly pinned; their lively spirit stifled in skilled hands. The pressure had begun, and it would not stop until perfection was achieved. I could see what was ahead: decades and decades of pressure. I felt tears welling up in my eyes. No longer was it a nameless young bride sitting in that chair; it was me. I could see so much of my twenty-six-year-old self in that rigid posture. I wanted nothing more than to take 1997 Rachel by the hand and guide her away from the disapproving mirror and hairdo vigilante. I wanted to wrap my arms around my impressionable, young self and whisper words of love and assurance. I wanted to spare myself from years of unnecessary pain and pressure by divulging something that took me nearly forty years to discover. If I could, this is what I would've told my younger self:

"You are going to feel a lot of pressure in your lifetime—pressure to do things at one-hundred-and-ten-percent performance level, pressure to look and act a certain way, pressure to be all things to all people. You're going to think that the pressure is coming at you from all directions, but in most cases, it's not. That unrelenting pressure is going to come from one place: you. So do yourself a favor, dear one. Take the pressure off. Take the pressure off now—don't wait until you're forty. In fact, don't wait another day."

When I was twenty-six, I was already contemplating what momentous achievement I would accomplish by my fortieth birthday. There were thoughts of running marathons, climbing high peaks, earning a doctorate, teaching at a prestigious university, and let's not forget being so fit and youthful looking that people would mistake me for someone in her early thirties. But something got in the way of that plan. I began my Hands Free journey. And the closer I got to my fortieth birthday, the more I realized that the best gift to myself (and those around me) would be freedom from self-induced pressure. More than an attractive appearance, more than press-worthy triumphs, more than a glowing reputation for being able to *do it all*, I wanted to live each day well. I wanted to live *today* well. And one surefire way to do it was to create my own definition of success. Capturing a sunset with my eyes ...

reaching out to someone in need of encouragement ... coveting precious pockets of time to spend with the people I love ... putting my complete trust in God ... expressing gratitude for life's simple joys like fresh air, belly laughs, and worn-out treads on running shoes ... these were just a few of the daily "successes" I experienced that cultivated more joy than any trophy ever could. By taking the pressure off myself, I was able to celebrate *ordinary achievements* that were really quite extraordinary when I stopped to delight in them.

When my fortieth birthday finally rolled around, I had fulfilled none of the aspirations I'd planned when I was twenty-six. I did what I'd been longing to do for many, many years. I went down to my basement and pried my long-undisturbed wedding dress off the clothing rack where it was smashed inside a mass of winter coats. My daughters had begged me for years to try on the adult-sized princess dress that glimmered in a dusty corner. My response was always the same: "No, not today." I knew my dress wouldn't fit, and for nearly all my life I'd been led to believe that a successful fitting meant the zipper went all the way up. But that was yesterday.

After slipping my arms through the beaded sleeves and taking a twirl for old times' sake, I walked upstairs to the room where Natalie and Avery sat watching television. When I entered, two small jaws dropped. Words of admiration spilled out and embraced me with the kind of unconditional love I'd deprived myself of for far too long. And when I turned to show them the back of the dress, I didn't even bother to explain why the zipper stopped right below my shoulder blades, refusing to budge the last few inches. The reason, or should I say reasons, my wedding dress no longer zipped closed stood staring up at me. My heart had grown two sizes since I wore this dress decades before.

As my past divinely merged with my present, I couldn't stop the tears. My daughters' hopeful faces confirmed that *Taking the Pressure Off* was the ultimate gift to myself and to them. I began considering the possible ramifications of living with realistic standards, as well as more meaningful ones, in all areas of life.

Questions like the ones below never failed to point me toward *ordinary achievement* rather than societal success:

> What if our self-worth wasn't based on the number on the scale but instead on the feeling of our body as it glides through the water?
>
> What if our happiness wasn't derived by our reading level but instead by the story within the pages of a book?
>
> What if our success wasn't based on the number of games won in a season but instead on the memories made and friendships created?
>
> What if our beauty wasn't determined by our resemblance to a photoshopped image but instead by our courage to have our own personal style and unique flair?
>
> What if our wealth wasn't based on how much we have but how much we give?

That would certainly be a Hands Free Life, wouldn't it? By rejecting societal measures of success, we open countless opportunities to grasp what really matters in a way that feels right in our heart and soul. Although it is not possible to go back and erase the pressure we placed on ourselves in years past, all hope is not lost. The words *not today* can be replaced with *why not today?* It's time we stop holding ourselves back from dancing, dreaming, speaking, loving, and living. Let's not wait another day.

Take the Pressure Off, the fourth intentional habit of a Hands Free Life, is an invitation to live by heart rather than by societal standards. From this perspective, you are able to find value in life experiences and outcomes that might otherwise be deemed failures or disappointments. As the weight of long-held pressures and unrealistic expectations lift from your mind, body, and soul, those around you will also reap the benefits of your newfound freedom. Even self-induced pressures have a way of contaminating the lives of those around us as much as our own. Just as you can heal from the damage of relentless past pressure, so can your loved ones.

In this chapter, we'll consider three ways to cultivate internal freedom. May you find that *Taking the Pressure Off* is a gift you can give yourself regardless of your current situation, age, or past reputation. May you find that the best rewards in life are not placed on the wall of your home but inside the lines of your heart.

To grasp what really matters, we must let go of what doesn't. When we begin to celebrate ordinary everyday achievements in our lives, something extraordinary happens: Life becomes richer. Hearts become fuller. Inner doubts become silenced. Smiles become wider. And no matter how the dress fits, you're still free to dance in the arms of your precious ones until your feet grow tired.

TAKE THE PRESSURE OFF SO OTHERS MAY TOO

I wasn't sure how Natalie would react to hearing me admit my most painful truths in a bookstore filled with friends, colleagues, neighbors, and complete strangers. Although Natalie had heard snippets of my past mistakes and the lessons I'd learned from them, this particular book-signing talk contained a steady stream of the most difficult admissions I'd ever spoken out loud.

Although I was concerned about how she would react to this complete baring of my soul, there was something that troubled me even more. Would she see herself in the pre–Hands Free version of myself? And if so, would this be good or bad? You see, Natalie and I are *very* much alike. Natalie is a planner and has the organizational skills to run circles around even the most ambitious adults. She is very busy, rarely sitting down, because there are so *many* ideas to bring to life. Natalie is a mover, a doer. With quick strides, she wastes not a single minute doing what her heart leads her to do. But when things don't go as planned ... or when perfection is not achieved ... or when the expectations she sets for herself (or others) are not met, Natalie is not a happy camper. Sayings like, "Everybody makes mistakes" only tick her off even more. There's no question where Natalie acquired these personality traits. She lived with me, her perfectionistic mother, for the first six years of her life. My highly driven, type-A tendencies had rubbed off and stuck like a regrettable tattoo.

The bookstore owner interrupted me from my reverie to tell me it was time to address the audience. As people took their seats, I saw Natalie break away from a group of friends. She was looking for a place to listen. My worry intensified. Would she hide her face in embarrassment? Or worse, would she make a beeline to the children's section and act like she didn't know me? No—she did none of these things. Natalie found a prime spot off to the left of my small author platform, away from everyone else. As I began to speak, she rested against the bookshelf as if planning to stay awhile.

With the most tender expression on her face, Natalie stood there captivated. And there I stood, exposing my flaws and the lessons learned, wondering only what one particular person was thinking about my confessions. There was this look on Natalie's face—the one that so many people noticed and later commented on as they came through the signing line—that gave me overwhelming peace. I couldn't deny the overpowering love radiating from one spot off to my left from a little girl with humongous brown eyes who was hanging on my every word.

Watching her mother take her imperfections and mistakes and turn them into life-changing revelations offered a reprieve to this mini high achiever. I saw the recognition take place on Natalie's face. The missteps of a messy, imperfect life were not something shameful or bad—they were a means to a more loving and fulfilling life.

Watching Natalie watch me was like seeing the sun come out after a long, hard rain.

Watching Natalie watch me was like seeing the tightrope walker realize the ground was much closer and much softer than he thought.

Watching Natalie watch me was like seeing a worn bandage taken off to reveal healing pink skin underneath.

In that moment, Natalie's radiant face was a reflection of my own—peace with who I was and hope for who I was becoming. But there was more. Her eyes seemed to sparkle with a possibility she hadn't considered before—maybe "It's okay to make a mistake" wasn't just a saying. Maybe it was actually true. This could be a turning point in her life, I thought to myself. With a little more guidance and a little more openness about past regrets, I could alleviate some of the future pressure Natalie was bound to put on herself. I vowed to speak to her in private to further encourage this shift in perspective that I believed was happening in my child.

"I am sorry I used to want things perfect all the time," I blurted out to Natalie in the glow of the night-light at *Talk Time* a few days later.

"Give me an example," she asked unexpectedly.

"Do you remember how stressed out I would get about wanting things to look a certain way when we left the house? Or how I made such a big deal out of trivial mistakes and mishaps?" I asked, bracing myself for distressing recollections.

"Not really," she shrugged. "I just remember how you used to lay out my clothes every morning, and I didn't get to pick. But now you let me wear what I want." She snuggled closer. "I like the way it is now."

"I'm so sorry, Natalie," I repeated. "I wish I would have realized sooner that relationships matter more than expectations, plans, and appearances. Pushing perfection on myself caused me to yell and become exasperated over minor things. It was hurtful to you and Avery, but it was also hurtful to me. My blood pressure was dangerously high back then. I felt angry a lot. My unrealistic expectations could never be met so I was constantly disappointed. I don't want to know how many perfectly wonderful days I ruined and how many feelings I hurt by putting pressure on myself. I wish I'd changed sooner," I admitted with regret.

"It's better to know it now than never know it at all," she wisely offered, taking my hand in hers. I closed my eyes and prayed such a mature remark meant she was starting to know it too.

The next morning Natalie's words were fresh on my mind as we prepared for school. Avery was standing in front of the mirror parting her hair straight down the middle. She completely ignored the back of her hair, and as a result, it resembled an angry cactus plant.

I could see Natalie eyeing her little sister's disheveled mess. She reached out her hand to take the brush, but then quickly drew it back without saying a word. Avery, unaware she was being observed, walked out humming to herself happily.

Natalie looked up at me. I was about to find out just how much our discussion the night before had resonated with her. "The old you probably would have fixed her hair, and she probably would've cried." After pausing for a minute she admitted, "I thought about telling her to change it, but then I decided not to say anything. It's better to just let her be who she is. People's feelings matter more than how things look," she said with certainty.

Natalie ran off to gather her backpack while I stood there relishing what had just transpired. As I stared at my teary-eyed self in a mirror splattered with toothpaste, the most beautiful thought occurred to me. Maybe second chances are not *given to us* but instead are something we *offer to ourselves* by using new words and new actions. And maybe the undesirable traits that were passed on to us and passed on to our children don't have to stick like permanent tattoos. Maybe they can be birthmarks instead—beautiful reminders that we don't have to live perfectly, but rather with small, positive steps and daily doses of God's grace.

 ## HANDS FREE LIFE DAILY DECLARATION

Today there might be mismatched socks. There might be not-so-healthy food choices. There might be messes, bulges, and fine lines where I don't want them to be. But today I will be at peace with my less-than-perfect day, my less-than-perfect body, and my less-than-perfect life. I refuse to waste precious time or hurt precious people (including myself) in my unachievable pursuit for perfection. After all, love doesn't have to be perfect to be nurturing or nourishing.

TAKE THE PRESSURE OFF TO LIVE LIFE FULLY

"I want be on the swim team like Natalie," Avery announced shortly after she turned six. She'd even put on Natalie's team suit and Speedo goggles to show that she meant business. The suit was drooping in the rear and the goggles were on upside down, but this was no laughing matter. In fact, this was cause for celebration. Standing before me was the girl who'd let out agonizing cries whenever her hair was washed for nearly her entire life. The bath-time hysterics had only stopped a few months earlier when she witnessed her baby cousin get soaped and rinsed while wearing a smile. "Please, please, please can I join the swim team?" begged my guppy wannabe, who no longer had an aversion to water.

"You'll have to get your head wet and swim laps," I clarified. It felt it was important to point out that swim team wasn't just playing cards, eating Twizzlers, and chugging Gatorade like she witnessed many swimmers doing at her sister's meets.

Avery *did* understand what being on the swim team meant and actually breezed through the initial evaluation to swim the length of the pool without stopping. In just a few short weeks of practice, Avery was demonstrating proficiency in the various strokes and kicks—and always with a smile. When it came to diving off the block, however, the situation quickly deteriorated. (Cue the quivering lip and tearful protests of hair washing gone bad.)

For weeks, Avery's coaches patiently spent time coaxing, encouraging, and trying everything short of bribery to get her to dive off the blocks. Finally, one momentous day, she did it—but it was a fake-out. Although she'd looked fully prepared to enter the water in appropriate dive form, her entry turned into a feet-first jump as soon as she left the block.

While this imperfect dive might seem acceptable to the average observer, official swimming guidelines deem this practice unsafe. Avery was informed that because she was not *dive certified*, she was not permitted to dive off the blocks in the upcoming swim meets. Thinking this restriction probably made her feel sad or different,

I offered to work with her on a headfirst dive. Her eyes instantly filled with tears. "Mama, it's too scary to look down into the water and think of my head going before my feet," she cried. "Can I just keep jumping in from the side?" she asked hopefully.

Before my Hands Free journey, my response likely would have been a sharply delivered, "Well, if you are on the swim team, then you need to learn to dive properly." (After all, what would people think?) Before my Hands Free journey, I would have insisted Avery keep practicing, despite fear and tears, until she dove properly from the blocks. Before my Hands Free journey, I was far too concerned about what "other people" thought. I wanted my children to keep up with everyone else's children. I wanted it to appear as if we had it all together. While traces of my inner competitor/perfectionist still remain part of who I am, I knew this was not the time to force my child into doing something she did not feel comfortable doing. This was a time to *let go and let be*. I knew that Avery would become dive certified in her own time. And if she was content to begin her competitions by jumping off the side, then I should be too. Little did I know the impact she would make when given the freedom to decide when and how she would break the surface.

Our family had driven an hour to attend a large swim competition that included several other YMCA swim teams. After a quick warm-up, it was time for Avery's twenty-five-yard freestyle event. She stepped toward the blocks with the other competitors. As the other girls climbed onto the blocks, she stepped onto the edge of the pool where she was accustomed to doing her *Fake-out Dive Jump* into the water. Avery extended her arms so they covered her ears and was in dive position waiting for the start buzzer.

Suddenly, the official held up his hand and told the girls to relax. He said something to Avery's coach. Scott and I nudged each other. We knew this delay had to do with our child—the freckle-faced girl with unruly curls peeking out beneath her swim cap. I could see the official shaking his head. He was telling Avery she was not permitted to dive off the side. Through hand gestures,

I could see he was giving her two choices: dive off the block headfirst or start from the water.

After approximately ten seconds of careful consideration, my daughter made her choice. And when she did, I had an unexpected emotional reaction. Warm, silent tears began dripping down my face. My daughter did not climb on the starting block and make the dive of her life. Instead, she gently slid herself into the water. After giving one last look up at her competitors standing high up on their respective platforms, she gripped the side of the pool. With one hand extended, she was ready for takeoff. When the buzzer sounded, the other girls dove in and Avery pushed off the wall with all her might. As she propelled herself to the other side of the pool, I could not stop the tears, nor did I try. Despite a tumultuous start, my child was smiling. I could see that joyful, goggle-clad face each time she turned her mouth for air. No interpretation was needed. *I am on the swim team just like my big sister*, that enormous grin said.

After reaching the end, Avery hopped out of the pool and briefly conversed with the lane timer. Her eyes scanned the crowd looking for me. I was already heading her way. As my child walked toward me, I swear she looked taller. Stronger. More grown up. My new hero walked toward me.

It might seem odd. I write this story as though some grand achievement occurred. If I were to view this experience using twenty-first-century standards of success, there is nothing noteworthy here. My child did not win her race or any of her other three events that day, nor did she dive from the blocks. But I didn't view this experience through the eyes of mainstream society; I viewed it using a Hands Free perspective—and that makes all the difference, a life-changing difference.

What I witnessed in the water that day is the essence of grasping what matters in an environment that can so easily sway you to focus on what doesn't matter. Forever etched in my mind is Avery sliding herself into the water as anxious onlookers looked at their watches and tapped their feet. Their annoyed facial expressions revealed their inner thoughts: *Get on the block already. We don't have all day.*

How easy it would have been for Avery to say, "I am not good enough."

And walk away.

How easy it would have been for her to declare: "I am not a real swimmer."

And refuse to try.

How easy it would have been to shamefully hang her head in defeat.

And give up.

How easy it would have been to miss an opportunity to shine.

And never try again.

But Avery did not take the easy route. Instead, she courageously did what she needed to do to participate. That meant rejecting the pressure to do what everyone else was doing and do what was comfortable to her. Avery may not have dove in headfirst, but she gave it her all. She didn't let an unusual entrance ruin a perfectly good swim, a perfectly good meet, a perfectly good day, or a perfectly good life. *Suddenly this child's moment of weakness became her moment of unimaginable strength.*

By witnessing this moment of unconventional triumph, I garnered four truths that I refer to whenever I feel the need to conform, to push, or to pressure others or myself:

1. Living life fully takes courage—you must be willing to do things differently than everyone else.
2. Living life fully is not in the first-place finish, the shiny blue ribbons, or the flawless form; it's in the joy you feel in your heart because you were brave enough to try.
3. Living life fully doesn't require diving in headfirst, sometimes it means getting your toes wet to see what you are made of.

   And finally ...

4. Living life fully means becoming an unsuspecting hero to those who mistakenly let perfection sabotage their happiness—because if you haven't heard the news: Happiness beats perfection. Every. Single. Time.

Just watch the happy kid in the swim cap.

She is living proof that it takes an imperfect dive to fully embrace every drop of your glorious life.

HANDS FREE LIFE DAILY DECLARATION

Today I will use words that I hope will echo in my loved ones' heads in times of challenge and failure: *I love you exactly as you are. You are worthy of love and kindness. There is nothing you can do to make God love you any more than he already does. I am happier simply because you exist. You are more than enough to me.* Today I will be a voice of courage and encouragement to others, including myself, even if the words feel awkward coming from my lips. Today the voice of pressure and perfection will not prevent me from taking the chances I've always been too afraid to take.

TAKE THE PRESSURE OFF TO EMBRACE GOOD ENOUGH FOR TODAY

On occasion, I am interviewed via Skype about establishing healthy boundaries between technology and life. While I love sharing the Hands Free message with new audiences, live interviews are my least favorite way to share it. I much prefer writing about it so I can tweak my sentences until I get them smooth and flawless. Not to mention, when I'm delivering messages from my keyboard, appearance is not a factor. My writing "uniform" consists of comfy Dri-FIT workout clothes, socks that may or may not match, a Life is Good ball cap, and a ponytail sticking out the back (hair brushing optional).

I have no doubt that my preference for writing over public speaking has been influenced by the years I spent pursuing perfection, namely pressuring myself to sound and look just right. For every self-deprecating message I said to myself, a wound was left on my spirit. That wound deepened to the point that I declined social gatherings if I did not like my reflection in the mirror. My wound deepened to the point that I refrained from sharing my thoughts and ideas if I feared they would come out wrong. My wound deepened to the point that I shied away from living, laughing, and pursuing my dreams because I compared myself to others and believed I wouldn't measure up.

But somewhere along the line, those wounds began to heal. Instead of looking at myself through critical eyes, I began to see myself through loving eyes, namely the eyes of my child. I am not certain I would've realized the extent to which this new perspective saved me had it not been for an unexpected day at home with Avery.

On the morning I'd agreed to do a television interview via Skype, Avery needed to stay home from school because of a sore throat. The day before, she'd tested positive for strep. With two doses of amoxicillin in her system she was feeling pretty good, aside from a little discomfort when she swallowed.

"So what are we gonna do today?" asked my pajama-clad daughter with a toothless smile. "I love having alone time with you," she added genuinely.

I explained that I had a television interview at eleven o'clock, and I needed to spend some time practicing what I was going to say. I told her I would also need to shower and put on something a little more presentable. As I spoke, I waved my hand over my ultra-comfy, creative-thinking attire, assuming Avery would agree that my appearance needed improvement.

"I think you look good enough for a television interview," said my child who would wear her pajamas in public every single day and use a brush once a week if she were allowed.

I chuckled at her wise and empowering "good enough" perspective, which she offered as an invitation to play.

"How about a game of Connect Four?" she asked hopefully. "Remember, you were the Connect Four champion of your family when you were little." I am pretty sure she threw out that last bit knowing her competitive mother could never turn down a challenge.

As she hoped, I glanced at the clock and said yes. I figured I could play a few rounds and still have time to prepare for my interview. Connect Four was not nearly as riveting as it had been when I was nine years old, but there was something about sitting across from a child with disheveled hair and joyful eyes that made me lose track of time.

Suddenly feeling a little behind schedule, I told Avery I really needed to prepare for my interview. I set her up with a box of crayons, a blank notebook, and a glass of ice water. She quickly got busy on a full-page artistic creation.

I reviewed my interview questions only once. My inner perfectionist, who is known to butt in when I am trying to be Hands Free, forced me to consider reviewing them again. Yet Avery's earlier words squelched the voice of pressure. *It's good enough for today*, I thought to myself as I put the notes away.

I took a quick shower and put on the first outfit that appealed to me. Again, I hesitated and wondered if I should try on something else just to be sure this was the best option. It only took a quick glance at my favorite violet purple shirt and freshly washed hair to embrace Avery's wise mantra once again. *Good enough for today.*

I walked out of my bedroom intending to use the remaining few minutes to prepare for the interview, but Avery had a notebook full of drawings she wanted to show me. "Here's a picture of you. I messed up on your hair, but that's not what's important," she declared with conviction. Avery's portrait of me instantly confirmed my decision not to spend one more minute on that stubborn piece of hair that was determined to stick straight out. In my current state, I closely resembled the happy lady in the picture who held a yellow star in her hand—not a hairbrush.

Before I knew it, it was time for the Skype interview. I'd

placed a few sticky notes around the edge of my computer as "cheat sheets" but found I didn't need them. The news anchor was warm and friendly and had excellent questions. I found myself talking to her about my journey with ease.

At the end of the interview, I shut my laptop with a sigh of relief and satisfaction. To my surprise, Avery jumped out from around the corner where she had been listening quietly. "You did great, Mama!" she exclaimed. "Now let's go out to lunch!"

I considered saying, "Not today." I had a slew of writing deadlines to meet and more editing to do on my book, but I didn't. It wasn't every day that I had a lunch date—especially one with a toothless smile. I said yes to Avery's suggestion, and within the hour we sat across from each other enjoying the midday fare at her favorite restaurant.

Our attentive waitress noticed when our plates were empty and unexpectedly presented a brownie sundae to Avery. My typically chatty child couldn't even speak. All she could do was laugh and laugh and laugh with giddy delight. I took a moment to contemplate the reason for Avery's eruption of pure happiness. I came up with four possible explanations:

1. Because it is fun to be out to lunch when you are technically "sick."
2. Because the sight of ice cream with sprinkles just makes a person deliriously happy.
3. Because the waitress's unexpectedly kind gesture made Avery feel special.
4. Because she felt the overwhelming love coming from her mother sitting on the other side of the table.

I can't be sure why Avery was so happy in that moment, but what happened next left me with no questions about how I wanted to live out the rest of that day and the days ahead.

The waitress, who had turned to leave, stopped midstride. Despite having food orders to take and empty glasses to refill, she paused to listen to the sound of Avery's uncontainable laughter.

TAKE THE PRESSURE OFF

Suddenly, the woman put her hand over the heart, looked up to the sky, and cried out, "Thank you, Lord! That laughter is coming straight from the soul! Straight from the soul! And it's a mighty beautiful sound!"

As if on cue, Avery took the first bite of her succulent treat. After swallowing the icy-cold goodness, she looked completely surprised. "My throat doesn't hurt anymore! It's healing, Mama! It's healing!" she declared so loudly that people around us looked over and smiled too.

I had to fight back my tears as the significance of the waitress's words and my daughter's declaration suddenly hit me. My bruises, the ones made by years of critical torment, are healing too. Because each time I let go of *perfect* and allow myself to show up as is, the bruises on my spirit fade a little more. In that moment, I felt God's divine confirmation for the changes I'd made in my life and for the messages he continually places on my heart that are meant to be shared.

Let's stop pressuring ourselves.
Let's stop comparing ourselves.
Let's stop being our own worst enemy.
Let's stop holding ourselves back from life.

Instead, let's see ourselves through the eyes of those who love us . . .

Eyes that see beautiful when we cheer at the ball field with sweat-laden faces and tear-stained cheeks . . .
Eyes that see beautiful when we soothe away bad dreams in a fossilized college T-shirt with sleep-deprived eyes . . .
Eyes that see beautiful when we're rocking our bathing suit and slicked-back hair as we twirl our children's relaxed bodies in the pool . . .

When our loved ones look at us, they don't see flaws and imperfections, they see love—sweet, beautiful, never-failing love. When God sees us, he doesn't see a disappointment, he sees his beautiful child worthy of love and grace. May our eyes be opened so we see can see it, too. We can start today. When you find yourself going down the damaging path of criticism or comparison, try this freeing line: *Good enough for today.*

Just that one little change in thought can provide the courage to:

Show up,
Speak out,
Grab a star,
And laugh until tears run down your face.

See yourself through the eyes of those who love you. And let the healing begin on your wounded soul.

 ## HANDS FREE LIFE DAILY DECLARATION

To focus on what really matters, I will use one or more of these phrases today:

My time and effort on this project are good enough for what I am trying to accomplish.

My appearance is good enough for those who love and cherish me.

My house looks good enough for a home where life happens, children live, and mistakes commonly occur.

My contribution to the school/church/neighborhood event is enough to show my support and make a difference.

Embracing the words "good enough for today" is a way to free my loved ones and myself from the constraints of unnecessary pressure and unrealistic expectations.

HANDS FREE LIFE HABIT BUILDER 4

Take the Pressure Off by Making Today Matter

Today I hope to take a few extra seconds to kiss the top of your head before you go.

Today I hope to stand aside and let you do it yourself … even if it takes a little longer … even if it's messier … even if it's not perfect.

Today I hope to say, "I'm sorry" and "I love you" because they are life-changing, comforting, and healing words.

Today I hope to laugh more than I sigh with exasperated breaths.

Today I hope to view missed shots and off-key notes as brave attempts at living rather than failures to succeed.

Today I hope to focus less on your faults and more on your freckles and sense of humor because they light up your face.

Today I hope to notice the color of your eyes when you speak to me.

Today I hope to listen to your words without judgment and impatience.

Today I hope to extend grace for accidental spills and other human mishaps.

Today I hope to give you a little extra time to walk along the edge of the curb, do your own hair, and listen to your words.

Today I hope to remember you are more than your achievements, more than your academic performance, and more than your behavior.

Today I hope to catch a glimpse of you that suddenly reminds me how much of an extraordinary miracle you are.

Today I hope you go to bed knowing life is better because of you.

Today I hope you fall asleep feeling loved right now, just as you are.

Today matters. Today is all I really have for sure. Let today be a day I can look back on, whether in tragedy or joy, and say today was not perfect, but it was memorable. Why? Because I encouraged. I smiled. I listened. I apologized. I waited. I cared. I tried. But above all, I loved … oh how I loved … I loved myself and I loved the people in my life. Isn't that the best part of living—to love and be loved? I think so.

I will show it by making today matter.

It is easy to get caught up in the pressure—pressure to get promoted, to be financially successful, to have winning games, to be at the top of the class. Such pressures cause us to think ahead to tomorrow, next month, next year, and so on. How easy it is to forget about taking one day at a time. I'm guilty of letting future events matter more than what's happening right now. And while it's important to be prepared for tomorrow's spelling test, next week's staff meeting, next month's championship, and next year's grade level assessment, we must not allow these future events to matter more than what really matters now: Today. Today really matters. Today is all we know for sure that we really have.

Habit 5:

SEE WHAT IS GOOD

◄——— ❤ ❤ ❤ ———►

I want to see beauty. In the ugly, in the sick, in the suffering, in the daily, in all the days before I die, the moments before I sleep.
Ann Voskamp

I DIDN'T KNOW WHEN I'd changed from a positive person to a negative one; I only knew that I had. I could still remember myself as a cheerful special-education teacher, somehow managing to see the positives in every student and every situation, no matter how dismal. But somewhere along the line, I stopped seeing the goodness. I focused solely on what was wrong and what needed to be changed. Given the fact that I had a loving husband, two beautiful children, a healthy mind and body, and a safe and comfortable home, you would have thought I'd wake up every morning feeling grateful, optimistic, and content. But that was not the case. I woke up feeling the same way I did when I went to bed the night before—unhappy, annoyed, and irritable.

Like a robot, I could *speak* of my life's abundant blessings, but I could no longer see or feel them because I was too focused on my life's abundant distractions. Too many commitments. Too many screens. Too many self-induced pressures to be all and do all. Too many unachievable standards. Too many to-dos and never enough time. Too many balls in the air, not enough hands to catch them.

My outward discontent seemed to peak when it was time to leave the house. Although they were young, Natalie and Avery braced themselves for my daily departure tirade. While I fussed and fumed getting everyone ready and out the door, Avery grew very quiet. Natalie tried to help any way she could, assisting her slow-moving sister with her shoes, gathering snacks in Ziploc bags, and wiping stray cereal pieces from the kitchen counter. Of course, through my critical eyes, her helpful attempts only made it take longer and were never good enough. I didn't try to hide my exasperation or annoyance.

It shouldn't have come as a shock when I looked in the rear-view mirror to see Natalie anxiously picking her top lip as I pulled out of the driveway one morning. As she pinched that tiny piece of fragile skin on her upper lip with wide eyes, I could practically read her mind: *Mommy's mad. Mommy's tired. Mommy's stressed.* But there was more. I could practically hear how a young child would interpret her mother's unhappiness: *Mommy's mad at me. Mommy's tired because of me. Mommy's stressed because of something I did.*

All at once, I could no longer deny the damage my negative approach to life was having on my family. All the excuses I'd made for being harsh and direct, for constant faultfinding, and for being in a foul mood suddenly held no credibility. While choosing to emphasize every "problem" of my blessed life, I'd funneled my discontent straight into my daughter's once joyful heart and spirit. The pain on her face was a direct reflection of the expression I wore on mine. I said a tearful prayer right then and there, asking God to show me one small step I could take to bring back our lost joy.

A few days later we were just leaving our neighborhood to head to school. As usual, I'd corralled everyone into the car in a frenzied rush. But instead of barking orders and angrily pushing on the gas to arrive on time, I remained calm in light of my earlier prayer.

"Look up," a little voice inside me urged. I took my foot off the gas pedal and leaned forward to peer through my windshield. As far as my eyes could see, the sky was filled with a million little white clouds. It was as if a heavenly baker had taken an icing bag and decorated the sky, one sweet puff at a time. Although I knew the carpool line at school would be closing in five minutes, it didn't matter. I pulled the car over to the side of the road. I needed to show my daughters what it looked like when the morning sky decided to stay in bed, covering itself in an ivory quilt stitched by divine hands. I reached back and opened the sunroof cover above their heads. "Look up," I said, repeating the same words I'd heard a few minutes before.

Both girls looked up in unison. Natalie let out a little gasp. "I love it! I love it!" she exclaimed, as if I'd just presented her with the ladybug Pillow Pet she'd been eyeing for six months. Avery clasped her hands together and let out a joyful squeal.

I decided this unusual sky was a sight worth capturing. As I placed my camera at just the right angle, I found myself letting out a little gasp, just as Natalie had moments before. I couldn't believe what I was seeing. There, at the forefront of this magnificent sea of clouds, was the most perfect little handprint on the glass through which my daughters and I peered. Knowing her mother liked things clean and tidy, Natalie asked, "Are you going to wipe the hand off, Mama?"

"No." I shook my head, trying not to cry. "Never," I whispered, knowing something extraordinary was taking place inside me in that moment. "Isn't it beautiful?" I asked, knowing the girls would both look up at the glass again, and I could stretch this unforgettable moment out a bit more.

As my daughters looked up and marveled at the handprint against a backdrop of floating clouds, I noticed all our faces matched. We were all smiling. *Smiling.* This unique little imprint, found in the rarest of places, served as a divine sign to look harder, look longer, look deeper beyond the mess, mistakes, and mayhem to see the goodness. I was certain God was telling me this is where I would find joy again.

The fact that I did not wipe that handprint away became significant as I strived to see the blessings over the inconveniences. I quickly realized much of what aggravated me was trivial. Much of what was supposedly "ruined" were things that could be fixed or cleaned up. What mattered—that we were safe, healthy, and alive—were thoughts that began to overpower the negatives. But learning to see the positives in situations and surroundings was only the starting point of viewing life through Hands Free eyes. Seeing the positives in people (particularly characteristics that had once been perceived as weaknesses) was the epitome of living and loving fully and freely.

Rather than viewing Natalie, my eager-to-please, helpful older child, as "always getting in the way," I began to appreciate her willingness to jump in and assist. At last I could see her for who she was—not an annoyance or a bother, but a loving child with clever thoughts and ideas. Instead of focusing on the mammoth-sized mess she made while engrossed in cooking and art projects, I emphasized her creativity, passion, and drive. Avery, my stop-and-smell-the-roses younger child, was no longer viewed as a time waster, but rather my teacher for living mindfully. I learned how to grasp joy simply by watching Avery put on her favorite pair of pajamas and plant apple seeds in the backyard. The way Avery shrugged off mistakes and didn't have a worry in the world became my inspiration instead of my headache. Even characteristics I'd longed to change in myself were beheld with more loving eyes. My sensitive side, which I hated for being thin-skinned and introverted, was what enabled me to *feel* life. I finally realized it was that part of me that allowed me to write what others felt but couldn't express. Like that dirty handprint on the glass, I was able to see *unwelcomed* qualities as something at which to marvel, instead of to abolish. As it became a daily practice to see goodness in the most unsuspecting places, the tightness in my face disappeared. The lip-picking behavior in Natalie ceased. Smiles became common occurrences in our daily routine, even at departure time.

See What Is Good, the fifth intentional habit of a Hands Free Life, offers a chance to look beyond the outer surface to the heart of what matters most. It is a perspective that allows us to see beyond our distractions, our hang-ups, and our preconceived notions to see the blessings right in front of us. *See What Is Good* allows us to be an encourager rather than a dictator ... an original rather than a conformist ... a bearer of joy rather than a messenger of gloom.

In this chapter, we'll consider three examples of how seeing the blessings in people, situations, and events can bring great hope and direction to our lives and the lives of people we love. May you find that it *is* possible for gratitude to overpower the negative. By making it a daily practice to *See What Is Good*, the joy in your heart has the tendency to overflow. And when it does, you are able to funnel that excess happiness straight into the hearts of those you most want to see smile. Even in the most dismal situations, even in times of challenge, even when the whole world sees something that needs to be changed, you can see what is good, and you can protect it from being wiped away.

SEE WHAT IS GOOD TO NURTURE INNER GIFTS

I'd waited six years for this moment. It was the confirmation for which my worrisome heart had yearned. Natalie's small hand shook nervously as she held the microphone. Standing in front of our entire church congregation, Natalie described how she chose Pricilla, the girl with the broken smile, from an array of children in desperate need of education, friendship, and hope through a Compassion International sponsorship. Natalie concluded her inspiring speech by adding, "You too can put a smile on the face of a heartbroken child like I did."

It was all I could do not to grab the microphone from Natalie's hands and yell, "Wait! There's just one more thing!" And with conviction, I wanted to look into the eyes of every parent in the audience and say these words:

"Someday, maybe tomorrow, maybe a year from now, someone

will tell you that your child has an issue, a problem, a weakness. Someone will tell you your child needs to be changed. But before you attempt to stifle that issue out, I beg you to look at the flip side. Take your child's 'problem' and look at it from the other side. With the right nurturing and encouragement, that weakness might turn into your child's gift. And to deny it, alter it, or extinguish it could have tragic results. I know this because someone once told me to change the very heart of the child who just stood here and told you how to save someone else's life."

Natalie's early years were a blur. A colicky baby, an active toddler, and a traveling husband successfully wiped entire days from my memory bank. But there was one day from Natalie's early years that I will never forget. Natalie was nearly three at the time; her unique personality was already beginning to take shape. She was an attentive caregiver of stuffed animals. She comforted other children when they got hurt. She was kind to all creatures, even the unsightly roly-poly bugs that lived in the cracks of our driveway. But most of all, Natalie loved singing and dancing and going to Miss Beth's music class on Tuesday mornings.

Normally Natalie stood up the entire class period laughing and smiling, but not on this particular day. On this particular day, her face was buried in the front of my shirt. Natalie wasn't crying, but she was hurt. She was sad. She was offended.

Another child had aggressively grabbed the musical instrument she had been playing with from her small hands. As I comforted Natalie, I could feel a penetrating glare coming from the mother sitting next to me. In a disapproving tone, this woman I considered a friend chided, "All I can say is you need to toughen that child up." And if that wasn't enough, the woman then predicted a dismal future with a shake of her head. "Because if you don't toughen Natalie up, she is going to have a very rough life ahead of her."

I drove home from music class in a state of worry. I envisioned a grade-school-age Natalie hiding beneath the playground slide from the bully who taunted and teased her. I envisioned

Natalie as a young woman unable to ride the subway for fear of the hungry eyes that hovered over her as she boarded. It was true; my child's feelings were easily hurt, and yes, she was extremely tenderhearted, but did this mean she needed to be changed? Did this mean she was doomed for life? Did this mean I needed to start "toughening her up"—as if such a process even existed?

I reflected back on my former special-education students who had severe behavior disorders. I remember how their parents desperately longed to see one tiny shred of compassion or kindness in their children who hurt animals, other children, and themselves. Perhaps that is why when I looked at my overly sensitive child, I saw something most people didn't. I saw compassion, altruism, and kindness in my thin-skinned daughter.

When Natalie and I got home, I did something highly unusual for an insecure young mother whose copy of the book *Healthy Sleep Habits, Happy Child* had a yellow sticky note on virtually every page. I made a declaration based on what I saw when I looked at my child, not what someone else didn't see. Staring into my child's big brown eyes, which held so much promise, I declared, "I will never, ever 'toughen you up.' Mark my words. Someday, someday that tender heart inside you will be your gift."

Six years later *someday* arrived. I was given not one but two confirmations that seeing my child's weakness as her strength freed her to become who God created her to be.

CONFIRMATION 1

When Natalie was asked to speak to our church congregation about her experience sponsoring a child through Compassion International, she was hesitant. The thought of speaking in front of so many people made her nervous. At first she said no, but after thinking about it awhile, Natalie changed her mind. Knowing there would be thirty available children who needed to be paired with a sponsor, she said, "I bet hearing a child talk about helping a child will make more people want to do it than if an adult talked about it." I remember hoping and praying she was right.

Natalie stood on a little step stool to reach the microphone. In her favorite blue-and-white flowered dress she told the attentive audience that when she was seven, she walked to the back of our church to a table filled with photos of children in need. Among a multitude of angelic faces beckoning her to pick them, Natalie chose the unsmiling Pricilla. Natalie remembered exactly what she said when she lifted up that picture of the pitiful-looking little girl and so did I. "I want to give her a reason to smile," Natalie told the congregation.

Natalie explained how she wrote to Pricilla many times, hoping for a letter or a picture that would reveal the status of Pricilla's smile. Soon one came. Natalie described the photo of Pricilla, her mother, and a social worker standing around a basket of fish that they were selling to pay for educational materials. The enclosed note said Natalie's latest donation had helped buy those fish. "Most people would have looked at that picture and wouldn't have seen a smile," Natalie said. "But I did. Pricilla's lips were curved up a little bit. She was smiling a little more than before," she announced joyfully.

At the end of the service, fifteen families flocked to the table at the back to choose a child to sponsor. By the end of the week, all thirty children were adopted. Through Natalie's gentle and compassionate ways, she motivated others — children and adults — to do something they perhaps wouldn't have done. She encouraged them to make a difference, to change someone else's life. This was the first confirmation I received that seeing and nurturing Natalie's "weakness" enabled her to fulfill her potential. That was enough, but yet there was more. Confirmation 2 came a few weeks later and put my worries about Natalie's sensitive heart to rest indefinitely.

CONFIRMATION 2

I was cleaning out Natalie's backpack at the end of a chaotic week. After pulling out a half-eaten sandwich and an unnecessary number of mini hand sanitizers that smelled like cupcakes, I saw a crumpled piece of notebook paper. It was a speech she'd written and recited to her class before being voted class president in a mock election. It read:

> My name is Natalie. Here are some reasons you should vote for me. I am hard working. I am very kind. I take care of the animals and the plants. I have self-control. I am very brave and honest. I am caring and a little curious. I am very smart and fun. I make a good leader. I care about other people. I am so exided to be one of the class presitents. Please vote for me.

I read it three times, and then I wept.

I cried for every little boy whose parents are told he is too rambunctious, too inquisitive, too loud.

I cried for every little girl whose parents are told her head is in the clouds, that she is a daydreamer and too much of a free spirit.

I cried for every little boy whose parents are told he is too small, too weak, and too timid to ever play the game.

I cried for every little girl whose parents are told she is too clumsy, too uncoordinated, too slow to ever succeed.

I cried for the mother who was told her child needed to be toughened up and for every year that mother waited for the moment she'd know that nurturing her daughter's tender heart was the right thing to do.

The moment was now. And there was cause for celebration. Not because I had been "right." Oh no — there was something much more miraculous to celebrate. In the act of noticing, protecting, and encouraging that overly sensitive heart at age three, my child's God-given gift had blossomed. And far more important than the fact that the world could see and appreciate her gift was the fact that *she* could see it herself, among the other gifts she possessed.

I shuddered to think if I had tried to change her, mold her into something she was not. What would I have destroyed in my compassionate child? I was certain she would have never written these words, her purpose, her future in clear legible letters. Therein lay the flip side to an overly sensitive heart, and it was a beautiful sight to behold.

As I reflect back on that life-changing choice I made early on in Natalie's life, I can't help but wonder what would happen if we stop trying to change the perceived weaknesses we see in one another. What would happen if we choose to look a little deeper, take a new angle, or just wait and see? Perhaps by celebrating each other as is, there would be fewer feelings of isolation, failure, inadequacy, and shame. Perhaps there would be fewer school shootings, fewer suicides, less road rage, less self-harm, and less despair. Perhaps if we were to look into each other's eyes and say, "I see you. I love you. You are exactly as God intended you to be," there would be more peace in our hearts.

Let us remember that weaknesses have a flip side; they have the potential to become strengths. It only takes one person to take something others see as a negative to mold it into something that can change the status of a smile, the status of a life, and maybe even the status of a child's future.

 ## HANDS FREE LIFE DAILY DECLARATION

Today I will step back and let my loved ones do things their own way ... in their own time ... with their own flair. Today I will step back and let them be who they are. And perhaps when I do, I will see something I thought needed changing doesn't need changing at all. Perhaps I will see something courageously brave and beautiful that is worth protecting and nurturing. Perhaps I will finally see their true colors, and I will rejoice.

SEE WHAT IS GOOD TO GAIN PERSPECTIVE

Summer. Just the word alone brings peace to my bones. *Summer.* It's morning sunshine, cool pools, warm oceans, bare feet, and extra scoops of ice cream. Summers are the much-needed exhale after nine months of school-year breath holding. But even the most wonderful things can lose their luster. There is a distinct difference between the *beginning* of the summer and the *end* of the summer. As wet towels, lost goggles, and long miles cramped in the family vehicle accumulate like sweat beads under your armpits, summer can quickly lose its initial glow.

That was precisely my state of mind when my daughters and I pulled into the parking lot of a local recreation center for an end-of-summer sports camp. "Nothing like being early," I told my daughters, who were grumbling in the backseat about being the first ones to arrive.

Donned in neon-orange shirts, the camp counselors beckoned the girls with friendly smiles and waves. Unlike me, the counselors looked rested, caffeinated, and enthusiastic. It could have been the sunlight coupled with the one-hundred-percent humidity, but to my weary eyes, it appeared they had halos over their heads. Walking on air, I led my daughters to the check-in desk. After filling out the necessary paper work in record time, we said our good-byes. I was eager to break free and sit in complete silence for a few hours. At this point, being able to hear my own thoughts nearly sounded like a tropical getaway.

Once I arrived home, I worked on a few articles that were soon due. After that, I made an effort to clear a path through the house. When I did, I couldn't help but notice my children's trails—or as I like to call it, "Kid Evidence." I noticed the way Avery had carefully arranged the shoes in her makeshift dollhouse ... the way her ukulele pick was placed right where she could find it ... the way she had gingerly set her glasses back on the second shelf when she came home from the movies. Among the disarray in Natalie's room, there was a notebook tossed on the floor and open

115

to a pretty decent drawing of her beloved cat, Banjo. The way she drew a hundred little hairs on his tail made me smile.

I hadn't noticed these things earlier, because when the kids are underfoot, these tender, little details tend to disappear. But in my children's absence, I could see them clearly. And these tender minutia made me feel happy and grateful.

After a day of writing to my heart's content, I went to pick up my children, but I didn't go right in. I wanted to see if they were having fun, making new friends, and getting along. I stood at the window of the gymnasium and watched for a few minutes. It was a free-play period with kids doing a variety of activities. I quickly spotted my daughters in their neon Nike shorts and sun-bleached strands of hair spilling from their ponytails. They were doing wall handstands with two other girls. Everyone was taking turns and helping to support wobbly legs if necessary. My girls were laughing, not bickering as they had been doing that very morning.

Suddenly my heart softened. Suddenly the long summer looked brighter. Suddenly I saw all that was good. And I knew where I was standing had a lot to do with it—this view from afar made all the difference. I dug into my purse until I found one of the small notebooks I keep handy in case writing inspiration comes unexpectedly. I wrote, "trails, mess, whining. But my days are better with you."

Perspective

Suddenly I had it. Because sometimes you have to step away to get it.

A few hours later, this is what came of those scribbles in my little notebook ...

PERSPECTIVE

Empty popsicle sticks sealed to the coffee table,
Cereal bag ripped open so the entire box spills out when I
   pour it,
Your tired face is not a pretty sight.
Bickering with your sister,

Forgetting to shut the car door,
Forgetting to flush,
Tags itch on the new shirt so you won't wear it,
Someone's been using my new lipstick again.
You can be stubborn, grouchy, messy, and exhausting.
But despite it all,
My days are better with you.
Because no one says my name quite like you.
No one else insists on a hug before I leave.
No one else has freckles in the exact same spot as me.
No one else's lips feel quite like yours on my cheek.
No one else can make me laugh until I almost wet my pants.
No one else waves like you do when I'm spotted from afar.
Your flaws fall away in the light of your perfect love.
My child, my days are better with you.

That was the perspective I got the day my children went to camp—but that wasn't the end. This shift in perspective continued, eventually covering larger, more sacred territory that included my own imperfections and strengths.

Shortly after camp concluded, the girls started school. On the very first day of school, I got that feeling. You know the feeling like you're forgetting something? Well, I felt like I was forgetting something because I *was* forgetting something. I'd forgotten to put money in the lunch accounts on the first day. I'd forgotten to sprinkle Avery's pillow with the glitter her teacher had given us for the night before the first day of school. I'd forgotten to sign up for the first swim meet. On top of all that forgetting, I had to be away for the night due to work.

In the motel room that night, I tossed and turned. I couldn't sleep because of the negative commentary going on in my head. I knew such talk was taking me down a damaging and useless path, but my failings were getting the best of me. I couldn't wait to get home the next day, vowing to do a better job of staying on top of things.

Natalie greeted me the minute I walked in the door. Although

117

she was getting more and more independent every day, she still didn't like me to miss her nightly tuck-in. She hugged me fiercely. "I slept with your special pillow last night," she murmured into my chest.

I was quite surprised. "My pillow?" I inquired, unconvinced that among the array of pillows that lay on my bed, she knew I had a favorite.

"You know, the one that is super floppy in the middle—the one that Daddy tried to throw out because he said it was gross."

I smiled. Yep, that was the one.

"It smells like you," she divulged.

Sure enough, when I tucked her in that night my droopy pillow was placed where hers usually sits. Embarrassingly, I noticed my lifeless pillow had several drool stains and needed a good washing. But these details did not offend my daughter. She snuggled her face right into it and inhaled deeply. "Ahhhh ... smells like Mama."

In an instant, my inner bully, the one that spews negative comments about my parenting failings, was silenced. And my shift in perspective continued to expand to include myself.

PERSPECTIVE CONTINUED . . .

No seconds on ice cream,
Shoes required when we go grocery shopping,
Your mad face is not a pretty sight.
Insisting on cleaning my room,
Bad morning breath,
Bad car singing,
You call me by my sister's name.
You have hairs on your chin.
Someone's been organizing my closet again.
You can be forgetful, impatient, and overly concerned with
  cleanliness.
But despite it all,
My days are better with you.

118

Because no one says my name quite like you.
No one else insists on a hug before I leave.
No one else has freckles in the exact same spot as me.
No one else's lips feel quite like yours on my cheek.
No one can make me laugh until I almost wet my pants.
No one else waves like you when I am spotted from afar.
Your flaws fall away in the light of your perfect love.
Mama, my days are better with you.

With an expanded perspective, I've come to this conclusion:
Let us not beat ourselves up if we have to be away—whether it is for work, pleasure, or just to sit with our own thoughts in the corner of Starbucks. Let us not feel guilty if we know we must put some space between ourselves and the ones we love the most. Why? Here are three reasons:

1. Because sometimes we need to step away to distinguish between what is truly important and what is trivial in the grand scheme of life.
2. Because sometimes we need to step away from the people we share our life with to see how beautiful they are.
3. Because sometimes the scent of a drool-stained pillow or the sight of a carefully placed stuffed animal in the absence of our loved one gives us what we need: *Perspective*—that moment when the flaws within yourself and the people you love fall away because your perfect love for each other overpower them all.

HANDS FREE LIFE DAILY DECLARATION

Today I will view the messy trails in my home as sacred evidence that living, loving, creating, and growing are going on here. If I choose to look at the clutter and disarray with a soft, open heart, I can see the quirks, hopes, talents, and dreams of my loved ones in these sacred trails. Although it is often imperfect, exhausting, messy, and monotonous, it is my life. And when I open my eyes, hands, and heart fully, what truly matters can outshine the mess.

SEE WHAT IS GOOD TO BECOME A NOTICER

Avery handed me her fall progress report. It displayed a steady stream of happy check marks in all the positive boxes. There was just one check mark standing dejectedly alone from all the others.

"How am I doing, Mom?" my child asked with a level of maturity that did not match the small disheveled person gazing up at me through smudged eyeglasses that teetered on the end of her nose.

I looked at her. Her flyaway hair and dirty knees indicated it had been a good day at school. I looked back at the progress report, then back to her again. Her face, lovely and round, still held traces of baby—unlike Natalie's face, which had suddenly elongated into an adult-like oval without so much as a warning. Finally, once more, I glanced back to the progress report and the one lonely check mark.

Before I consciously realized I'd made a decision, my face broke into an encouraging smile. I gathered my child into my arms and pressed my lips against her silky, smooth cheek. Before I spoke, I briefly closed my eyes and offered up a silent prayer of gratitude; she had come so far in a year's time. "You're doing great. You're doing just fine." I whispered into her ear, my voice containing a mixture of emotion and happiness. I decided I would not say anything about the low check mark or the words written beside it. This was just something that didn't need to be said right now . . . or perhaps ever.

But this child, with her bright blue eyes and sassy rose-rimmed glasses, misses nothing.

"What does that say?" With her small pointer finger, she tapped the neatly printed words that flowed out from the check mark that sat apart from the others.

Inside my head, I read the words: *Distracted in large groups*. But I already knew this. I knew this before it was written on an official report card. This news was no surprise to me. You see, each day this child comes home with an astute observation:

"Max has a group of warts on his right knee. There are exactly nineteen. I counted them."

"Miss Stevens got a new haircut. She got layers put in. It looks really pretty."

"Miss Evans eats Greek yogurt every single day. I think her favorite flavor is peach because she brings that one a lot!"

"Sarah is a wonderful artist. She can draw butterflies that look like they could fly off the page!"

And outside the school walls, it's no different.

"That waitress sure is working hard. We should leave a little extra money on the table."

"That man is texting and driving. He is going to hurt himself or someone else."

"Grandpa is slower than the rest of us. We should wait."

"Look out the window, everybody! Look at the gorgeous view!"

Distracted or observant? Distracted or perceptive? Distracted or empathic? I choose observant . . . perceptive . . . empathic.

"What does it say, Mama?" My child was growing impatient to learn the meaning of those words she could not yet read herself.

My children know I will always give them *truth*, even when the truth can be difficult or uncomfortable to say or hear. So I read her teacher's comment word for word: "Distracted in large groups."

My daughter gave a tiny, uncertain smile and shyly put her hand to her mouth. "Oh yeah. I do look around a lot."

Before Avery could feel one ounce of shame or one iota of failure, I went down on bended knee and looked her straight in the eye. And then I spoke the following words with every ounce of conviction I could muster; I didn't want her to just *hear* these words, I wanted her to *feel* them.

"Yes. You do look around a lot. You noticed Carter sitting off by himself with a skinned knee on the field trip, and you comforted him.

"You noticed the little girl who couldn't quite get up on the haystack at the pumpkin patch so you boosted her up.

"You noticed Banjo had a runny nose, and the vet said it was a good thing we brought him in when we did.

"You noticed the boy at the zoo looking lost and you suggested we help him.

"You notice the beautiful, breathtaking view every time we cross the bridge.

"And you know what? You've taught me to notice. And I don't ever want you to stop noticing. That is your gift. It is your gift that you give to the world."

By the look of bliss on her face, you might have thought she was just given unlimited access to a candy shop. She was literally glowing. *Glowing.* And even when she tried to suppress her smile and look serious, she couldn't.

"Okay, Mama. I won't stop noticing," she said solemnly, yet unable to contain her smile.

Along this Hands Free journey, we are required to make choices in order to grasp what really matters. These choices are not always the popular ones; they are not always status quo. These choices may be looked down on by outsiders and rejected by the "experts." But after you make these choices—they feel right in your gut—there is always validation. Sometimes this validation takes days, weeks, even years, but it comes. And when it does, you'll know you made the right choice for your child, for your family, for yourself. Thankfully, validation for the choice I made about the progress report came within days.

I'd just gotten my hair cut. It was shorter than usual. I was feeling a little insecure about it. I straightened it in such a way that was different from my usual style. I walked out into the living room, still in my pajamas, with this new hairstyle that I was not so sure about.

"Wow, Mama. You look so pretty! I love your hair." It was the voice of my observant child. My face relaxed into a smile, and I immediately felt better about my hair. Apparently my child could sense her words comforted me. What she said next stopped me in my tracks. "You were just waiting for someone to notice, weren't you?"

My hand covered my mouth to suppress my awe and my joy. I looked to the sky with tears in my eyes. Yes. *Yes.* We are all just waiting for someone to notice — notice our pain, notice our scars, notice our fear, notice our joy, notice our triumphs, notice our courage.

And the one who notices is a rare and beautiful gift.

Let us all be Noticers today.

Let us notice our children's gifts rather than their flaws.

Let us notice what our spouse does right, not what he or she did wrong.

Let us notice the sacrifices our parents made, rather than all the times they messed up.

Let us notice how hard people are working, not how quickly they are providing service.

Let us notice where our love and kindness is needed, rather than spew criticism and scrutiny where it is not needed.

Let us be Noticers. Love others *right* where they are. Love others *just* as they are. Someone is just waiting for us to notice what's blooming or wilting inside that could use a little undivided attention.

HANDS FREE LIFE DAILY DECLARATION

Today I vow to notice the good before the bad … the right instead of the wrong … the blessings above the inconveniences … the strengths rather than the weaknesses. Focusing on the positive is the key to finding joy in the most unsuspecting places and in the most challenging times. Today I will notice the good. Bring on the joy!

HANDS FREE LIFE HABIT BUILDER 5

See What Is Good with Glimmers of Goodness

Thank you, hurried morning. It is in the hunt for shoes, library books, and backpacks that I appreciate the slow Saturday. I shall pay attention and appreciate the Slow Saturday.

Thank you, perpetually cluttered house. It is in finding rumpled sheets, toothpaste blobs, and abandoned socks that I appreciate the evidence of life being lived. I shall pay attention and appreciate Life Being Lived.

Thank you, growing older. It is in finding another gray hair and another laugh line that I appreciate the gift of another day. I shall pay attention and appreciate the Gift of Another Day.

Thank you, free-spirited child. It is in experiencing everything a little faster, a little louder, and a little riskier that I appreciate the courage it takes to be bold. I shall pay attention and appreciate Being Bold.

Thank you, sensitive child. It is in experiencing everything a little deeper and a little more quietly that I see the beauty of a tender heart. I shall pay attention and appreciate the Tender Heart.

Thank you, pang of guilt. It is in wishing that I did things differently that I appreciate the opportunity of Second Chances. I shall pay attention and appreciate Second Chances.

Thank you, disappointment. It is in experiencing letdown that I appreciate the fact that I had the courage to try. I shall pay attention and appreciate the Courage to Try.

Thank you, daily challenge. It is in looking straight into the face of sorrow, struggle, fear, frustration, heartache, and worry that I appreciate the fact that I keep showing up. I shall pay attention and appreciate the fact that I Keep Showing Up. And I will keep showing up.

Because even on the hardest days, even in the most challenging moments, I can see tiny glimmers of goodness if I look closely for them.

So today I shall pay attention and appreciate any Glimmers of Goodness I can find.

Having a full and complete day of goodness is hard, maybe even impossible, considering life's daily stresses of children, bills, schedules, deadlines, responsibilities, and pressures. But finding Glimmers of Goodness within a day is possible—even when you are irritated, annoyed, or frustrated. In fact, it is in times of overwhelm that I can find these bright spots most easily. It may sound odd, but try taking each not-so-pleasant experience or feeling and thanking it for its hidden gifts. From that place of gratitude, you might be able to find a Glimmer of Goodness, reminding you that the whiny, messy, unpredictable moments of life are not all bad. In fact, they are what make home a home and a life a life.

Habit 6:

GIVE WHAT MATTERS

← ❤ ❤ ❤ →

Sometimes when you sacrifice something precious, you're not really losing it. You're just passing it on to someone else.

Mitch Albom

IT'S PROBABLY SAFE TO assume that at some point during your life, you've been given a gift from a child. It's probably also safe to assume that the gift was not from a shopping mall or even put in a box with wrapping paper or ribbon, but simply presented with love. In my case, broken seashells, traumatized frogs, bouquets of dying weeds, and handfuls of rocks were presented to me in small, dirt-laden hands beneath a wide smile. Those were just a few of the unconventional gifts Natalie gave to me throughout her first years of life. At the time, I considered her offerings of homemade gifts endearing and did not try to dissuade her. But as she grew, her gift-giving practices expanded to people outside the family, and that's when things got a little uncomfortable. I literally cringed at the sight of my child tearing through our kitchen junk drawer looking for the "perfect gift." When she found it, she would beam at the broken snow globe or the used neon Sharpie as if she just knew the recipient was going to love it. Teachers, pastors, neighbors, and friends were bestowed with gifts found in the deepest, darkest, dustiest crevices of our home. While some people may have viewed her regifting practices as earth friendly and generous, my inner perfectionistic, appearance-minded self could only think of the words *tacky* and *cheap*. I'd try to convince Natalie that she should shop for a gift with actual money, but she would have none of it. That wasn't special, she'd tell me. I would end up attaching a store-bought gift to her homemade offering until one winter my Hands Free heart told me to stop, watch, and learn.

Early that December, Natalie asked if we could make a holiday care package for a family in India with whom we'd connected through Samaritan's Purse. On top of the new pajamas, packaged toothbrushes, and pristine white socks, she placed two hairbrushes that she and Avery had used for almost a month. Despite my protests, she was adamant that the brushes must be included. Shortly thereafter we received a thank-you note from the family with an enclosed picture. You can only guess what the children were holding proudly in their hands. You only can guess who immediately noticed shiny, silky hair where tangles and knots had once been. You can only guess who sighed with relief and exclaimed, "Boy, I sure am glad we sent hairbrushes!" I decided I must keep watching and learning.

Around Valentine's Day we heard that one of my mother's friends had lost her husband of forty-seven years. I suggested we send flowers. Natalie assured me a handmade Valentine, created by her, would mean much more. In response to my daughter's card, the eighty-year-old widow wrote:

> Thank you for the Valentine. I thought I was not going to get one this year for the first time in many, many years. It made me sad, but now I feel better because I no longer have to worry about being forgotten. Always remember that some people have the ability to smile on the outside when they are hurting on the inside. These are the people who may need your gift of kindness the most. I know this for a fact because I am one of them.

As I read that dear woman's note, my idea of a "proper gift" flew right out the window. But it wasn't until early March, when a nasty flu season held on for dear life, that I made the critical connection between real giving and living Hands Free.

Natalie's best friend, Catherine, suddenly acquired a dangerously high fever and couldn't get out of bed. Within minutes of hearing the news, Natalie made a card and retrieved a beaded bracelet from the bottom drawer of our bathroom. I remember feeling slightly relieved that the price tag was still on the pearly accessory. By the end of the day, however, I was powerfully reminded that the cost and the condition of the gift were insignificant compared to the thought behind it. Catherine's mother called to tell me how much Natalie's present meant to her daughter. When the mother recounted what her child had said about the offering, I could not hold back my tears. With sincerity Catherine had remarked, "I bet a lot of people heard I was sick, and after they said, 'That's too bad,' they just went on with their life, but not Natalie. She stopped what she was doing to show me she cared about me. She's the best friend anyone could have."

I remember struggling to swallow the lump in my throat when I heard Catherine's profound observation. I quickly got off the phone and ran into the bathroom so no one would see me cry. Finally, I was ready to admit why my child's gift-giving practices irritated me so much. Yes, I liked presents to be new and nice. Yes, I liked to make a good impression on people. Yes, I liked to stay in line with the way mainstream society gifted, but the real truth was much more shallow and much more painful. The truth was, Natalie was willing to give something I wasn't. Her gifts were so meaningful to others because she put time and thought into them, and those were commodities with which I was not so generous. I was faced with an unsettling question: Could I really say I was living Hands Free if I didn't ever give the gift of myself?

I vowed to find a way to give meaningfully, thoughtfully, and habitually the way Natalie did. I narrowed my aspirations to one of my strengths. I could gift words. I decided that whenever I felt appreciation, concern, or love for someone, I would make a point to tell him or her either verbally or through a written note. For nearly two years, regardless of time, schedule, and inner doubts, I dedicated a few minutes each day to express love to at least one person. It wasn't until my family was about to move to a new state that I learned the impact of this purposeful offering. I'd posted a picture of the moving van on social media and told local friends to stop in for a hug if they felt inclined. I was shocked to see which neighbors came to my door and what they remembered most. One person said she would not forget when I called her from the Whole Foods parking lot just after she had her baby to see what she needed. One neighbor mentioned the birthday card I gave her where I listed all her positive qualities. She said she couldn't remember being affirmed as an adult and it had inspired her to affirm other adults. Another friend recalled the time I stood in the driveway listening to her struggles as if there was nowhere else I needed to be. She said I followed up with a card, which she now kept in her drawer.

I finally understood the difference between the way I used to give and the way Natalie taught me to give. There was *standard giving*—giving with shiny bows, loaded gift cards, and elaborate gestures. And then there was *undistracted giving*—giving your time and attention on a regular basis so that it becomes second nature; so it becomes who you are.

Give What Matters, the sixth intentional habit of a Hands Free Life, means offering your most precious commodity, the gift of yourself, even when there are a million distractions and pressures providing you with reasons *not* to give. Such a way of life allows you to readily notice opportunities to make a lasting impression on others while empowering you to seize these opportunities. Because you are no longer held back by how a gift looks, its price, or whether or not it is "good enough," suddenly there are countless ways to bring joy to the lives of others as well as your own. When you live life *Giving What Matters,* you free yourself from hidden agendas and unrealistic expectations. You also eliminate future regrets that might sound like, "I wish I had told her ..."

or "If only I had done it sooner ..." *Giving What Matters* means you no longer wait for the proper day, a grand occasion, or the perfect moment to express how you feel about someone. You freely open your hands and heart and let love pour out when it is needed. *Giving What Matters* is a liberating approach to living fully in today.

In this chapter, we'll consider three ways to let go of societal pressures and inhibiting attitudes to experience the joy that comes from true giving. As children often show us, our most precious gift is the one given from the heart with a loving smile — no wrapping paper required. A listening ear, a lingering embrace, a word of encouragement, sustained eye contact, one-on-one time, or a helping hand have always been priceless gifts, but they are even more sacred now that our culture has become so rushed and distracted.

To give our most precious commodity, the gift of ourselves, we must let go of all that distracts us from what matters most. Perhaps the perfect gift is not in the *getting*, but rather in the *letting go*. Letting go of societal standards ... letting go of monetary expectations ... letting go of perfection ... letting go of consumer pressure ... letting go of the need to out-do, impress, or check off the list. Let us give like the heart of a child — presenting the best of ourselves as if we were a carefully picked dandelion bouquet held out with love.

GIVE WHAT MATTERS TO PLAY AGAIN

Apparently when you play an instrument from age five to seventeen, people think it shouldn't be kept a secret — especially the people who live with you. I'll never forget the look on Scott's face when my dad suggested that my sister and I "play our instruments" during a holiday visit soon after Scott and I were married.

Scott shot me a look of confusion and then annoyance. "Hello? You played an instrument for twelve years? Are there any other hidden talents you've never told me about?" he joked.

My sister's shiny silver flute and my wooden violin with beautiful detailing made an appearance that afternoon. I was surprised at how my fingers remembered their placement on that smooth, ebony fingerboard. But once I put the instrument back in the case, it stayed there for another ten years. It survived three interstate moves, always managing to find a place on the metal shelf in the basement where it sat undisturbed.

"Daddy said you played the violin growing up," my little songbird, Avery, said one day, eyeing the mysterious black case when we were in the basement gathering suitcases for a trip.

"Yes, but I doubt if I can even play anymore," I said, crushing any hopes she had of hearing me play. Avery's disappointment was palpable, but it wasn't enough to end several more years of excuses. *It takes too long to tune. The instrument is so old it probably doesn't sound good anymore. I think the strings are about to break. Maybe after I've had some time to practice.* And that's just a small sample of the many reasons I created to avoid playing my violin.

But eventually there came a day when I couldn't bear to give any more excuses. I saw those reasons for what they were: sad, pathetic, and no longer acceptable. I'd come to this realization when considering how I might give my family a meaningful gift for the holidays. The answer was easy because it had been haunting me for over a decade. I wanted to show them how I once made music and that it was not too late for me to make music again.

The exquisite handmade violin that had sat neglected in its oblong case for twenty years finally saw the light of day. I'd decided to create a practice calendar. After all, if I was going to make this instrument come back to life, I needed to set aside time to familiarize myself with the instrument. I needed to refresh my memory on tuning the strings, reading sheet music, and placing the bow and my fingers properly.

Each night after my children went to sleep, I went into my narrow bedroom closet to practice. Because I no longer had a music stand, I'd prop the sheet music I'd printed from the Internet against dusty shoeboxes. At first, the sound I made was quite disturbing. Where the bow once purred on the strings, there was now the piercing sound of a catfight. My inner doubt said, "Give up!" My inner perfectionist said, "You should really clean this closet instead." My inner taskmaster said, "Shouldn't you be making cookies for the neighborhood cookie swap on Saturday?"

I pushed the bow down harder to drown out the negative thoughts that were distracting me from what really mattered. Whenever I found myself questioning whether practicing my violin was a valuable use of my time, I reflected on what my daughters might someday remember about the holiday. Would they remember how shiny the floors were? Whether or not the Christmas cards were mailed out on time? How many homemade desserts lined the counters? Or would they remember that on Christmas morning, their mama played her violin. They'd always wanted to hear their mother play, and it sounded better than they ever dreamed it would.

After all the gifts were opened on Christmas morning, I announced that I had a surprise. I watched as my parents, Scott, Natalie, and Avery all looked at each other inquisitively.

What happened next made me so thankful that for the three days prior, I'd cut my workouts short, let laundry go unfolded, forgone curled ribbon on the gifts, and allowed the floors to collect dust so that I had time to practice.

I unlocked the violin case with a loud click. By the look on my family members' faces, I was opening the gates to a secret world in which they had been banned for far too long.

"Is that your violin, Mama? Are you going to play, Mama?" The girls peppered the air with eager questions. They were so excited they actually stood on their chairs as if Itzhak Perlman himself was about to perform. I simply smiled and let my instrument answer their questions.

I began with "Silent Night," which I knew they would recognize, and then moved on to "Greensleeves." I'd chosen that one specifically for my mom because it was my grandma's favorite. Just as I'd hoped, my parents cried, Scott beamed, and my children were delighted at the sight of me with my violin tucked under my chin.

As I stroked the handcrafted bow on the graying strings of my instrument, a familiar feeling of peace settled over me. For a moment, I felt as if I was back in the pale-yellow bedroom of my childhood. On shaggy green carpet, my music stand held papers dotted with black notes that beckoned me away from my adolescent worries. Difficult teachers, friendship drama, and insecurities about my physique all seemed to fade as I became engrossed in the act of making music. While playing my violin, I had no choice but to be present in that moment. I was not thinking of what had been or what was to come—it was all about the now.

I was genuinely surprised to find that the violin still had that effect on me, even twenty years later. The performance I gave for my family was far from perfect, but it didn't matter. I'd retrieved a gift I thought was no longer available to me; I'd discovered a way to stop time and find refuge from the worldly distractions and pressures once again.

A few days later my mom told me something about my younger self that I couldn't quite fathom. She said, "You know you haven't always been this driven, Rachel. As a girl, you got lost in the moment. You took your time. You were carefree. It wasn't until college that you became so focused on always being productive."

A chill ran up my spine. When I went to college was precisely when I stopped playing the violin. That is when I stopped "playing"—period.

But after a beautiful rendition of "Silent Night" amidst the awestruck expressions of my family and the tears of my parents, I'd discovered I had the ability to play again. It was just a matter of choosing to do so. This time, I'd made a good choice.

That Christmas day the floors were dirtier than ever. The food I prepared was not magazine-cover worthy. My hair was in a messy ponytail. But it didn't matter. That holiday my home held a joyful noise—one of laughter, love, and a squeaky violin. And for a brief moment time was ours, so we held it with loving care.

HANDS FREE LIFE DAILY DECLARATION

Today I will make time to play. I will delight in an old hobby or talent that used to bring me joy. If the voice of productivity tells me I am wasting time, I will say, "On the contrary! I am stopping to momentarily hold time!" And then I will knit, bake, garden, woodwork, paint, sculpt, dance, or sing until I am completely lost in a moment and my soul is refreshed.

GIVE WHAT MATTERS TO GIFT A MOMENT

The month before Scott turned forty, I began thinking about how we should celebrate his birthday. Early on, he made it abundantly clear that he did not want a surprise party. Actually, he said he wanted no party whatsoever. He specifically said he just wanted to spend time together as family. It sounded easy enough, but yet I knew that I would be sorely letting him down if I did not make his fortieth birthday somehow different than the thirty-nine birthdays before.

I wanted to make Scott's birthday special, but I secretly hoped I could figure out something that didn't require a lot of effort on my part. The sad truth was, I made a point to go the extra mile for just about everyone in my life, but I often "cut corners" when it came to my spouse. I banked on the fact that my husband would love me no matter what, which meant he got shorted on my time, effort, love, and attention. These truths are not pretty, I know. However, painful admissions such as these are the key to grasping what really matters on this Hand Free journey. So with that said, I give you more honesty. I decided a nice family overnight at a local hotel with a pool and amenities would make a unique and memorable fortieth birthday present. This gift idea had the appearance of a big deal, while requiring little effort from me, the giver. It was the perfect plan ... *for me, that is.*

I immediately made the hotel reservation, stressing to the receptionist that although my husband frequents their chain of hotels for business, it was imperative that they did not send him an email confirmation. I hung up feeling quite satisfied with myself. *Make special plans for Scott's birthday . . . Check!*

A few hours later my husband walked in the door with a puzzled look on his face. "Do you know anything about a hotel reservation for December second?"

Crap! (Or if I am being totally honest, slightly worse than *crap*.) I could not believe it. My surprise was ruined! Or shall I say, my "easy out" was ruined? I went straight to the phone, punching the numbers so violently that I misdialed three times. For the next thirty minutes, I traveled the hotel's chain of command until I got to the top, lambasting every poor phone representative along the way. When I finally got to executive director, Renee, beads of angry sweat glistened on my forehead.

"Do you know how many times I told your reservation receptionist *not* to send my husband an email confirmation?" I asked in a snarly voice that even I did not recognize.

Poor Renee. Of course she didn't know. All she knew was that she needed to get off the phone with this customer-service nightmare. Renee offered me some "frustration points" to rectify the situation.

Frustration points? That's putting it lightly! I thought. *What about "Our Hotel Messed Up a Brilliant Fortieth Birthday Surprise" points? I am going to need about 50,000 of those, and they'd better cover the cost of the room!* I lamented in my head.

At this point, I felt as if my head was about to pop off my body. I knew I needed to take a deep breath before I said something I would regret. That's when I caught sight of myself in a hallway mirror. I did not like what I saw. In fact, the sight of my puffy, irate face was so embarrassing that I wished I could rewind my life forty-two minutes and forgo calling the hotel. All this drama, nastiness, and anger over someone's innocent mistake? I don't think so. This epic meltdown was not about the accidental error made by the person who sent the hotel confirmation to Scott. This complete overreaction was about me! This was about the woman who was desperately trying to "cut corners" on her husband's fortieth birthday when she should be taking those corners, dipping them in chocolate, covering them in sprinkles, and adorning each one with a tiny gold crown.

As anger turned to tears, I knew it was time to acknowledge a few hard facts. I was blessed to be married to a man who would rather spend his fortieth birthday with his family than have a huge bash. I was blessed to be married to a man who would rather eat my smoked almond-turkey meatloaf on paper plates with his wife and children than be served on white tablecloths at Ruth's Chris Steak House. And most importantly, I was blessed to be married to a man who never ever cuts corners on me!

That's when I knew his fortieth birthday gift was going to be different than I'd planned. I was not going to take the easy way out on this one. His gift was going to require more than simply dialing the 1-800 number of a hotel chain. It was going to require more than presenting a credit card at his favorite store. This gift was going to be one that represented what really mattered—how Scott truly mattered.

I immediately sat down at the computer and wrote an email to every family member, friend, and work associate Scott had ever known. I informed them that he was about to turn forty and that I would like them to send me a memory of him—funny, serious, meaningful, or all of the above. Over the next few days, the email messages started pouring in. Although I know my husband very well, there are twenty years of his pre-Rachel life that I don't always know that much about. And although he is a good communicator, there are just some memories and facts about his life that do not come up in daily conversation. And although I love my husband deeply, there are redeeming qualities about him that I have not yet come to fully appreciate. So as the messages filled my in-box, I found myself learning amazing things about my husband that I didn't know. I found myself in awe of small gestures he had done for people that had profoundly changed their lives. I found myself hanging on every word, as if reading a biography about a truly kind and inspiring man. I found myself laughing out loud. I found myself wiping away tears.

When the deadline for memory submissions came, I printed the huge stack of responses, slid them into page protectors, and placed them in a binder. But before I wrapped the binder, there was something I knew I must do. I called Natalie and Avery to sit with me, and then I proceeded to tell them all about their daddy. I read bits and pieces of the loving, humorous, and meaningful messages that I thought the girls would understand and enjoy. They loved hearing how Scott had once worn pink as a baby. They laughed when they heard how his wooden-bat baseball league teammates called him "Scooter" because of the way he "scooted" across the field (a much kinder way of saying he ran slowly in his ripe old age). The girls delighted in knowing Scott had sent money to his little sister when she was in college, and he sent it with only one condition: to have fun with it. They laughed envisioning their daddy as a sixteen-year-old boy installing speakers in his car with a bass that nearly shattered the windows. Their faces grew solemn when they learned of the way he helped tornado survivors, inner-city kids in need of role models, and a friend with cancer. As Natalie carried the book to bed with her that night, I knew this gift was something that mattered.

On Scott's birthday our family gathered around the kitchen table, and I began reading a list entitled "Forty Things We Learned about Our Daddy." When we spoke of childhood tent-building with his cousins, my husband quickly looked surprised. "How do you know that?" he asked bewilderedly.

I kept reading and the children kept smiling, because he was about to be handed the most unexpected gift. When the list had been read, we presented the album and left him alone so he could read every thoughtful word written about him in silence. At one point, I peeked around the corner to see his reaction. Scott held the same look of happiness I'd seen on our wedding day and the same serene expression he wore when he'd held his children for the first time. It was a look that said, "Something divine has just touched my soul and filled me with peace."

The rest of the weekend was spent celebrating in a Hands Free manner I like to call *Going Where Life Is Simple*—running around the park in the sunshine, going for a leisurely walk, eating smoked almond-turkey meatloaf made from scratch, devouring cupcakes slathered in buttercream frosting, and getting lots of hugs from little hands. That night, as Scott drifted off to sleep, he whispered, "Thank you. This was my best birthday ever."

As I watched my contented husband fall into peaceful slumber, a chilling revelation struck me as I realized the full magnitude of his memory book. Such meaningful sentiments are not usually spoken about people until the day of their funeral. This means people never get to hear exactly what others love about them. They never get to hear how they touched someone's life. They never get to hear the words of gratitude someone always wanted to tell them. But by the grace of God, and every single person who wrote a message in Scott's album, my husband got to hear these significant words on the day he turned forty. And equally important, his children got to hear them too while their daddy was still alive to be celebrated.

As my eyelids grew heavy at the end of a memorable day, I thought of the one line from my husband's memory book that I'd tried to read aloud to him, but my voice had failed me. It said, "Scott Stafford never misses a moment." I smiled at the irony. What did I give my husband on his fortieth birthday? For once, I didn't cut corners. Instead, I gave him a moment. And it was the perfect gift ... *for him.*

HANDS FREE LIFE DAILY DECLARATION

Today I will make plans to gift an experience, a moment, or a memory to someone I love instead of a material item. I might ask my mom to show me how to make her famous apple pie. I might ask my dad to go golfing or fishing. I might offer to help my children make a fort in the backyard. I might offer to give my friend a manicure. Today I will *Go Where Life Is Simple* and invite someone to come along. Away from the distractions of everyday life, I am more able to say the words I often don't take time to say. I will not wait until unexpected tragedy to express my love and appreciation for the people in my life.

GIVE WHAT MATTERS TO EASE THE PAIN

An editor for a small magazine that featured stories about creativity, courage, and world change contacted me about an article I'd written about Natalie's uninhibited gift-giving practices. The editor hoped that Natalie herself would be interested in writing a piece that detailed how and why she gave. As I read the editor's message, the child in me became giddy. By the time I turned eight, I'd already filled ten Mead notebooks with poetry, narratives, and endless streams of words. As a budding author, nothing would have made my story-writing heart happier than to see my words in print. I wanted to respond to the editor with an enthusiastic yes, but I knew that was not appropriate. Just because this would have been my dream as a child didn't mean it was Natalie's. I hoped she would accept this unique opportunity, but I decided I would not pressure her. It would be entirely her decision.

That evening as Natalie was preparing for bed, I told her about the email I received from the editor of *Courageous Creativity*. As casually as I could, I asked, "Would you be interested in writing an article about why giving gifts makes you happy?"

Suddenly the head that was lost in a sea of flannel popped out of the hole in her pajama top. "Published ... like in a real magazine?" my daughter asked excitedly.

The word *yes* barely escaped from my mouth when Natalie jumped straight into the air and screamed, "I would! I would!" Without missing a beat, she eagerly asked, "Can I get started right away?"

Although it was close to bedtime, I was thrilled by Natalie's enthusiasm. I offered her twenty minutes to write. My eager little author ran to get a pencil and paper and then positioned herself next to me on the floor. Although it is my inherent nature as a former special-education teacher to instruct, guide, and make suggestions, I said nothing. This was Natalie's story, not mine. Therefore, I knew the words must be hers, not mine.

The two of us sat there in the peace of my child's lemon-yellow bedroom, each of us writing stories we couldn't wait to tell the world. My daughter began writing "Giving from the Heart" while I worked on a blog post. The twenty minutes flew by quickly, and soon it was time to call it a night. Reluctantly, Natalie agreed to work on her story a little more the next day.

After one more twenty-minute writing session the next evening, Natalie announced her piece was ready to be viewed. I was given the honors. Within the first paragraph, the teacher in me spotted a clearly stated main idea and thoughtful organization. I made a mental note to thank her third-grade teacher for the exceptional job she had done teaching my child how to write an effective narrative. I continued to read on, thinking there would be no surprises. After all, I was there the day my big-hearted child wrapped toiletries and used books in hopes of bringing cheer to homeless people in our city. But as I continued reading, I realized I didn't know everything. And what I learned changed my perspective of the world dramatically.

Natalie described driving into the heart of the city. Her story picked up where we saw hundreds of homeless people gathering for food distribution. I remember exactly how I felt in that moment. I was scared. I wanted to protect my children, cover their eyes and spare them from seeing such despair, desperation, and hopelessness. I remember thinking it was a bad idea to go there. But as much as I wanted to beg Scott to turn the car around, I didn't. And now with Natalie's profound words staring back at me, I was given confirmation that proceeding into that heart-breaking scene was the right choice for my child. In that moment, fear was the furthest thing from her mind. This is what Natalie wrote: "We were in the downtown area of our city when we drove past something I will never forget. Many homeless people were crowded around this broken-down truck. A man on the truck was holding up an orange, saying 'Merry Christmas' and throwing out oranges for hungry people to catch. When I saw people pushing each other to get to the oranges, it made my heart drop. They were fighting for a piece of fruit. That is how little they had. Beside the truck, I saw an old man, maybe around the age of sixty. He was eating one of the sandwiches and oranges given to him. I thought to myself, 'I want to help this man.' I quickly hopped out of the car, gave him a gift, and said, 'Merry Christmas, sir.' Earlier, he had seemed so gloomy, but as we drove off, I saw a smile. I felt so good!"

Suddenly it all made sense. After that momentous day downtown, Natalie's giving practices escalated. In fact, suddenly there was nothing my child owned that couldn't be given away. I would find packed boxes of her most prized possessions in the closet. She would explain the boxes by saying, "Next time we go to the Autism Center ..." or "Next time there's a tornado ..." I also noticed that after the oranges experience, Natalie made a point to carry dollar bills in her purse if we were going into the city. As we walked the busy streets, her eyes searched for a cup or hat in which she could place her hard-earned dollars and make someone smile.

I remember when Natalie called me to the computer one day to show me a video of a child and his mother who had to walk for hours to get water—water that was contaminated and dirty. As tears dripped down my face, my daughter consoled me. "Don't cry; there is a way we can help." Natalie proceeded to tell me all about *Water for Life* as if she was their smallest (and most convincing) spokesperson.

Natalie had always gravitated toward the world's suffering, always yearning to know the world in its truest state. Starting when she was very small, the recurring question at our nightly *Talk Time* was this: "Mama, tell me something bad that happened in the news today."

I remember looking into those somber brown eyes, knowing full well that if I didn't tell her, this resourceful child would find ways to see what was out there. So with reluctance, I'd explain in words she could understand about the atrocities that many faced, the dangers that lurked, and those who had lost so much. I'd stand by and watch her digest every troubling morsel I offered. Time after time, I worried that it was too much, too overwhelming, too disturbing. After all, the problems of the world are vast and insurmountable. At least that is what I used to think. But thanks to the heart of a child and God's gentle guidance, now I know differently.

That day when we drove into the city, my daughter saw with her own two eyes the world I'd spoken of—the one that could be cruel, hungry, desperate, and cold. But she was not scared. Oh no, she had been waiting for this moment, dreaming of this moment when she could do something to help. You see, her eight-year-old eyes did not look at that scene and see daunting global issues like poverty, violence, hardship, and hopelessness. She saw one man whose entire day could be brightened by a mere piece of fruit. *A mere piece of fruit.* And when you see something as painful and as beautiful as that, everything changes.

My child walked right up and stared directly into the eyes of suffering. She watched in awe as tears of joy collected in a man's eyes simply because of her unexpected presence on a dingy city street on a cold day in December. And from that moment forward, this child became a full-fledged giver. Because when you have the most important things in life—like love, faith, and family—there is nothing you own that you can't give away.

HANDS FREE LIFE DAILY DECLARATION

This week our family will plan a visit to a place where our hands can lift others—perhaps a domestic-violence shelter, a nursing home, a soup kitchen, or a poverty-stricken area of our city. I do not want to shield my loved ones from the struggles of humanity or the world's dark underbelly. I want to be the one my loved ones turn toward to learn about the pain and suffering in the world. Therefore, I will allow difficult truths to come from my lips in language they understand. By revealing the travesties occurring in our community and our world, several positive outcomes could result:

- my children's hearts will be led to help
- they will know they are not alone in their own struggles and pain
- they will gain appreciation for their life's abundant blessings

Many hopeful reactions can happen when I face life's atrocities side by side with the people I love.

HANDS FREE LIFE HABIT BUILDER 6

Give What Matters by Offering a Piece of Yourself

As my child and I slowly made our way back to dry land, her arms squeezed a bit tighter around my neck. She rested her cheek against my face as if to savor this moment and engrain it to memory. In that intimate gesture, I swear I could read her mind—not her present mind, but her future mind. I could practically hear the words she would say to herself one Sunday afternoon as she drove home from the grocery store or while she walked her child to school or while she stared at the ceiling counting useless sheep. This is what I heard my daughter's future mind say:

When I was one week shy of five years old, my mother carried me out
to the deep end of the ocean.
She held me as we talked about life.
I don't remember exactly what we talked about that day, but I
remember her long, wet hair secured in a ponytail that glistened
like a horse's tail in the summer sun; I remember how it felt silky
smooth as I stroked it in my hand.
I remember how her eyes crinkled up as she laughed and how her
smile lingered like the smell of the coconut sunscreen on her skin.
I remember how I was in charge of when we returned to the shore;
she didn't seem to have anywhere else she needed to go or
anywhere else she wanted to be.
I remember how it felt to be held in her arms as the gentle waves
splashed against us and occasionally graced our lips. Even the
salt water tasted sweet.
We were in the deep end of the ocean, but I was not afraid; I was in
my mother's arms.
The week before I turned five, my mother gave me a moment and
through that moment she has held me all along.

Avery doesn't remember the Polly Pockets or the stuffed animals she
received on her fifth birthday, but she still talks about going into the deep
end of the ocean with me that day. I try to remember this on birthdays,
holidays, or whenever someone needs a lift. When you offer a moment,
you offer a piece of yourself. And although you may not know it at the time,
the recipient holds tightly to that piece of you. And when the waves of life
come tumbling down, it is that piece of you that gives them the strength to
keep standing. I cannot think of a more valuable gift. Can you?

PART THREE

Protecting What Matters

Habit 7:

ESTABLISH BOUNDARIES

◄────── ⌄ ⌄ ⌄ ──────►

Things which matter most must never be at the mercy of things which matter least.

Johann Wolfgang von Goethe

MY FAVORITE BEACH ACTIVITY when I was a girl was to rescue live starfish that had washed up on shore. I couldn't bear to see the helpless five-pointed creatures withering in the sun. Regardless of how long it took or how many times I had to bend over, I'd put every washed-up starfish that I could find back into the water so it could breathe again.

But somewhere along the line I stopped saving starfish.

Actually, I can pinpoint exactly when it happened: my highly distracted years—when to-do lists took over … when the pace of my life was a constant mad dash to a finish line that couldn't be reached … when I gripped my devices tighter than the hands of my loved ones … when I said yes to everything requested of me *outside* the home and said no to the most important activities *inside* the home. Work, technology, and life bled into each other to the point that there were no longer any protected areas. Daily distraction was invited into the sacred spaces of my life. It didn't

149

matter if it was a moving vehicle, the bedroom, Saturday mornings, family vacations, or even the middle of the night—these times and places were all open to distraction's overpowering and damaging presence.

Needless to say, I walked past a lot of starfish during that time in my life. Who knows how many? But the day I finally *did* notice a displaced starfish deteriorating in the sand once again, I was encouraged. This particular beach walk occurred on my first family getaway since beginning my Hands Free journey. I was in the early stages of waking up from my distracted state and taking small steps to reduce the excess that consumed my life. I guess you could say *What Really Mattered* was on my radar that day.

As I ran along the flat sand, something caught my eye in a tide pool. At first I ran past it, but I just couldn't keep going—I had to go back. Peering into the stagnant water, I saw a small starfish that was missing a limb. It appeared to be dead, but I felt compelled to wade in and be certain. With urgency, I reached into the water and pulled the little critter out. I turned it over expecting to see no movement, but amazingly its tiny tube feet waved at me. I surmised that the poor starfish had been the partial snack of a small predator. Yet despite missing a ray, it was alive—and it was fighting to survive.

"Breathe," I whispered to the maimed starfish. "Breathe."

It suddenly occurred to me that tears were dripping down my face. I was not just talking to the starfish, I was also talking to myself. I knew full well that living in a tech-saturated, productivity-driven society without healthy work/life boundaries was a surefire way to wither and die. There needed to be places, times, and circumstances when I could breathe life into what mattered most. I was crying because I could no longer bear to watch the sacred areas of my life suffer from lack of attention, love, and space to breathe.

Stopping to place the fragile creature back in its natural habitat felt like divine confirmation to me. I took it as a sign that I was making progress on my journey toward a more present and fulfilling life. I wanted to continue supplying oxygen to the most important aspects of my life so they could thrive, not suffer. But as I watched the replaced starfish being tossed and turned by the churning sea, I couldn't help but wonder if my Hands Free aspirations were futile. Like that tumultuous body of water, the distractions of our culture have the power to derail us despite having the best intentions. We are continually tempted by the latest and greatest electronic gadgets and apps. We are inundated with work demands and volunteer requests. Everyday household duties seem to never end. While we may successfully overcome our distractions today, what about tomorrow? There is always another wave of diversions and pressures threatening to pull us under. "How can I protect my Hands Free Life with so much coming at me?" I cried. I stood at the edge of the water praying God would help both me and that starfish thrive despite the forceful waves.

Upon returning from the beach I wrote my first "viral" post. Within days of its publication, nearly one million people had read "How to Miss a Childhood." Many small newspapers and radio stations wanted to talk to me about the piece. But when NPR messaged me for an interview, my jaw dropped. Excitement bubbled up inside me as I considered the potential impact of a nationally syndicated show promoting the Hands Free movement. Before responding to the email message, I read it once more. When I got to the last sentence my heart dropped. The host wanted to interview me at five p.m. and that was my designated Hands Free time. At the beginning of my journey, I'd established media-free time from three o'clock until my daughters' bedtime. Natalie and Avery counted on that time with me. And on this particular Friday, I'd promised to take the girls to the opening of the neighborhood pool.

I stared at the email message contemplating my choices. For a moment I considered accepting the request "just this once." The people-pleasing achiever part of me didn't want to let anyone down or miss this unique opportunity to spread the Hands Free message; I knew full well this opportunity might not happen again.

"But what about the starfish?" a little voice inside me said. *Yes.*

151

Oh yes. Thank you, God. I thought. That starfish I'd saved at the beach represented the promise I'd made to my daughters. It also represented the promise I'd made to myself—to authentically live the message that I write. To keep that promise from dying, I had to protect it. Crossing the boundary line I'd established between work and life would open up the temptation to keep crossing that line until it no longer existed. I would quickly find myself back where I was before—overwhelmed, desperate, and unable to nurture what was sacred in my life.

I remained true to commitment and politely declined the NPR interview and asked if there was any other time that would work. There wasn't, but surprisingly, I did not feel as if I'd missed out. I felt triumphant that I hadn't missed what mattered most. Through the sweet smiles on my daughters' faces that day at the pool, I felt God's divine assurance. He gave me confidence that establishing and maintaining boundaries to protect the sacred parts of life would enable me to experience eternal rewards that far surpassed any worldly successes or accolades.

Establishing Boundaries, the seventh habit of a Hands Free Life, enables you to nurture the relationships, passions, values, and core beliefs that matter most to you. Healthy parameters provide the structure, motivation, and insight to say no to the things that can harm what is most precious to you. But be warned. *Establishing Boundaries* is not always easy. It means having to reject mainstream trends and expectations to be true to what you believe is in your best interest. It means having to stand up for yourself and make difficult decisions that may not please those who want your time, energy, and attention. Yet by creating limits on the excess that can flow into your life at any given time, there is space to laugh, live, love, pray, play, and breathe. *Establishing Boundaries* allows you to go to sleep at night knowing you did your best to protect your one precious life from the corrosive elements associated with worldly distraction and pressures.

In this chapter, we'll consider how to establish healthy boundaries and make difficult choices in order to grasp what really matters. May your eyes be opened to the ways you can instill protective parameters in your life regarding online activity, availability to the outside world, and word choice that fosters relational growth. May you be reminded that you have the power to save a life, a dream, a marriage, a childhood, or a friendship by establishing watchful barriers that reflect your values and personal life goals. What we breathe life and energy into will thrive; what we neglect and abuse will suffer. Let us draw a line in the sand, on the calendar, and in our own heart regarding what we are not willing to risk losing forever.

ESTABLISH BOUNDARIES TO PROTECT INNOCENCE

Like most kids today, Natalie was born with an inherent ability to navigate technology. While it took me many months and hours of tech support to learn how to manage an online blog, Natalie created a website in one afternoon. And after spending a year in Technology Club, Natalie's knowledge far surpassed mine and now seems to be more advanced than ever. This makes me proud ... and also scared.

As I watch Natalie delve deeper and deeper into a digital world so foreign from the one I grew up in, a little voice within me urges me to keep up. Although it takes great patience to listen to Natalie describe everything she knows about iMovie, computer programming, online games, and QR codes, I eagerly accept her invitations. I am grateful each time Natalie says, "Check this out, Mom," because I know the number of invitations will decrease as she grows. I accept her cyber invites knowing that while I sit beside her, I can gently dole out warnings of online dangers that don't come inherently but instead from experience and awareness. While Natalie expertly clicks and navigates, I educate her about online predators and warn her about giving out personal information. Natalie knows about the children whose innocent online "chat" with someone they thought was a kid turned into a grave and life-changing mistake.

Despite my best efforts to be an active participant in my children's online activities, there was still something missing. For months, an unsettling feeling nagged me each time either of my daughters was online. Unexpectedly, a unique opportunity came to my attention. A friend of mine was organizing a program to educate the parents in my community about ways to protect their children in the electronic world. The two-hour program was appropriately called "Innocence Lost." Using a forum-style setting, several experts in the field of technology safety would be providing specific ways to guard children from the dangers of technology. My first inclination was to think that Avery and Natalie (age six and nine at the time) were too young to be exposed to such risks. Thank goodness I listened to that little voice urging me to attend the program anyway. As soon as the first panelist began describing the dark and dangerous descent his life took after an accidental discovery on the Internet, I felt grateful I was there. I looked around the room knowing the parents sitting beside me had children ranging from toddlers to teens. Despite the differing life stages, I realized we are all here at the right time. Anytime a person opens his or her eyes to the dangers of the online world is the right time, I concluded.

Two well-spoken, highly educated young men described how they stumbled into the world of pornography and quickly lost everything that mattered most to them. Although their life situations and addictions were vastly different, I heard the following similarities in their stories: They'd wanted their parents to *ask* questions. They'd wanted their parents to be *involved* in their lives — including their online lives. They'd wanted to know they could come to their parents *openly* with any mistakes and wrongdoings and not be shamed or dismissed. I willed myself to remember what I heard: *Ask ... Involve ... Be Open*. As additional technology experts described an array of filtering and accountability software programs for all types of devices, I willed myself to remember two more invaluable actions: *Protect ... Educate* (both my children and myself).

Needless to say, I left the program disturbed and shaken but also aware, empowered, informed, and motivated. I would not put my head in the sand and allow the cyber world to corrupt my children's innocence. As if sensing I had something weighing heavily on my mind, Natalie wanted to know what the "Lost Innocence" program was about. She and I had opened up discussions about other heavy adult issues six months earlier, but this was my chance to tell her about pornography. This was my opportunity to tell her how these particular websites are designed so people immediately see disturbing images when they click on the site—even if they go there by accident. As an example, I told Natalie about a child who googled the name of a sporting goods store with the word "ball" and wound up seeing a sexually explicit photo. "The images of this nature are the kind that once you see them, you can't get them out of your head," I warned.

That's when an unmistakable look of worry and shame came over Natalie's face. My heart stopped beating for a moment and my mouth became dry. *I am too late*, I thought sadly.

"Is that what happened to you?" I forced myself to ask, although hearing her response was truly the last thing I ever wanted to hear. "You can tell me, honey. It's happened to me, and it's happened to lots of kids," I assured.

I soon learned that when she was a mere kindergartener, she was searching for American Girl doll videos. She saw one that had a doll on its initial cover image, but once she clicked on the video, she saw things that she knew were not appropriate ... things she knew were not for children ... things that made her feel bad and shameful.

I am too late, I thought again for one brief moment—she'd already viewed disturbing content and harbored feelings of shame. But before I let regret consume me, I quickly reminded myself of this hopeful truth: *Anytime a person opens his or her eyes to the dangers of the online world is the right time.* The words of the courageous young men who spoke at "Innocence Lost" came back to me in full force. *Assure your child he did nothing wrong. Assure your child what she saw doesn't make her "bad." Assure your children they can come to*

*you anytime they see or do something that makes them feel embarrassed,
confused, or upset.*

I told Natalie I was sorry I hadn't protected her from seeing
that video. I told her that her dad and I learned about filtering
software that we would be installing on all the devices and com-
puters in our home. I explained that this software would block her
and her sister from going to any sites they should not see.

As promised, we installed Net Nanny on all devices that very
night. When I saw how beautifully the program kept my children
from going to questionable sites that they might accidentally (or
purposely) go to, I wished I had done it sooner. I quickly reminded
myself that now my eyes were open. I was trying to do all I could
to *Ask ... Involve ... Be Open ... Protect ... Educate.*

As relieved as I was to have the software protection imple-
mented in our home, I had to acknowledge that this did not
totally eliminate the risk of my children seeing inappropriate
content on the Internet. There was still a good chance that their
friends would not have such restrictions on their devices or in
their homes. That is why I felt it was important to talk more
in-depth about the dangers and empower Natalie with additional
knowledge. In age-appropriate terms, I explained to her why the
pornographic sites were harmful and disturbing. We discussed
how they do not portray intimacy and sex the way God intended
it to be. We talked about some things Natalie might say or do if
she felt that she or a friend was getting into questionable territory
in the online world. We reviewed the definition of cyberbullying
and how intentions to tease or ridicule can end up taking a tragic
turn. I reminded her that she could come to me no matter what
she has done or no matter what has been done to her.

The "Innocence Lost" program reaffirmed my commitment
to model healthy device usage — to show my children that there
is a time and place for device usage and that a phone did not need
to be an added appendage requiring constant checking. Despite
my children growing up with technology ingrained in so many
facets of life, I want them to look back on their childhood and

remember holding something other than an electronic box. I want my daughters to remember holding our cat, Banjo; a wooden spoon to form cookie dough; musical instruments; books; bike handlebars; ladybugs; seashells; and especially my hand in theirs. Because my actions largely influence their actions, I make it a priority to exercise daily, go outside, and do things with my hands like baking and reading books. I always insist that my children join me in these activities. What is sometimes met with grumblings quickly turns into smiles because stepping away from technology just feels good.

A few days after Natalie and I discussed healthy technology usage, she came downstairs and asked me if she could call her friends to go on a bike ride. "I am trying to keep in mind how long I have been on my device. And it's time to take a break," she said.

I felt a surge of happiness. Granted, I knew that just because she was being mindful of her technology use that day didn't mean she would the next day. But Natalie's comment showed she was gaining awareness, which is essential to establishing healthy tech/life boundaries now and in the future.

I am trying my best to empower my children with the wisdom to make smart, safe, healthy, and informed decisions about their digital lives. I will admit that it would be a lot more convenient to just let my children go to a separate room and stare at a separate screen. And it would be a lot easier to let them figure it out themselves rather than delving into this cyber world that seems to change drastically with each passing day. But the cost of separate rooms, separate screens, and separate lives is high. Not being a part of my children's online world can lead to irreparable damage to their mind, body, spirit, and future plans.

The minute we hand our children a smartphone or a computer, we are handing them access to everything—good and bad—in the cyber world. But it doesn't have to be that way. *Ask ... Involve ... Be Open ... Protect ... Educate ... Model.*

Even when the words don't come easy ...
Even when they push you away ...

Even when you're tired after a long day ...
Even when you think this doesn't apply to your child ...
Even when you think you might be too late ...

The moment you decide to open your eyes to the dangers of the digital world is the right time. *Ask ... Involve ... Be Open ... Protect ... Educate ... Model.* Although it may seem a little foreign, these are six more ways to love and protect a child — twenty-first-century style.

HANDS FREE LIFE DAILY DECLARATION

Today I will begin thinking about how I can talk openly about the dangers of computer sex offenders and potential online dangers with my loved ones. I will spend time with my children online. I will ask them to show me their favorite online destinations, and I will express genuine interest in what they do there. I will create media-free zones in the house, such as the bedroom, and warn my loved ones of the dangers of sending photos or personal information to anyone online. I will install blocking software or implement parental controls. I will be open about why I must be privy to their email accounts, text messages, and online communications. I will make it my priority for my children to understand why they must never set up a face-to-face meeting with someone they meet online. Above all, I will make sure my children understand that I love them no matter what mistakes they make in the real world or the cyber world.

ESTABLISH BOUNDARIES TO PROTECT RELATIONSHIPS

Avery rushed upstairs, her face wet with tears. She's been playing Legos with Natalie. When she asked Natalie for help with a complicated section of the structure, Natalie cut her down — her demeaning words sharp and pointed and straight to the heart.

The condemning words Natalie said to Avery sounded

painfully familiar. It wasn't too many years ago that I was impatient, short-tempered, and critical in my interactions, especially to Natalie, because she was the oldest child. It made perfect sense that these same negative reactions would come out of her when dealing with her little sister, just as they had when I dealt with her. In addition, it seemed that as Natalie became more *tween* and less *child*, her patience grew thinner ... her sass stronger ... her tone edgier. And there was just something about her little sister's laid-back, leisurely nature that pushed Natalie's buttons. I knew that Natalie and Avery's vast personality differences were only going to become more dramatic as they aged. It was time to point out the invisible boundary line between what was acceptable in our home and what was not acceptable before irreparable damage was done.

I went downstairs to talk privately with Natalie. She was aptly securing the final pieces to an impressive Lego tree house. Pushing stray pieces aside, I sat down next to her. "I have something to tell you," I said, my voice low and serious. Natalie knew to stop fiddling and look into my eyes. "Whether you like it or not, you are shaping Avery's self-esteem. The way she feels about herself will largely come from how you treat her. In fact, your opinion of her may be even more important than mine."

I paused to let my daughter absorb this. When I continued talking, I surprised myself by divulging something I hadn't fully appreciated until that moment. "Do you know why I know the impact your opinion has on Avery's life?" My daughter shook her head. "Because I *was* the little sister. Yes, my sister and I fought over clothes, music, whose turn it was to feed the cat, the bathroom, and other silly things, but never once did Rebecca shame me or put me down. Not once. Just imagine what that gift did for me."

By now I was crying. Surprisingly Natalie wasn't looking at me strangely or searching for the nearest exit. With a mixture of interest and sadness, she looked like maybe what I had to say was something worth listening to. I swallowed hard, attempting to regain control over my unexpected emotional breakdown. "We all need someone in our corner, to have our back, to believe in us when we don't believe in ourselves. If you haven't noticed, your little sister looks at you like a hero. And when you criticize or belittle her, it hurts. But when you compliment or encourage her, she soars."

I informed Natalie of my expectations, which happened to sound a lot like my number one classroom rule when I was a teacher. At the beginning of each school year I informed my students that our classroom was a safe haven. While I fully expected there to be squabbles and disagreements between children, there would be no hurtful attacks on physical appearance, intelligence, or abilities. I told Natalie that this is how I felt about our home. "I expect you to treat Avery respectfully and kindly, no exceptions. I expect the same from her and will tell her so," I said.

I suspect there are some people who might think such expectations are unrealistic, impossible, or just downright ridiculous. "Siblings are supposed to knock each other down and toughen each other up," I can hear the naysayers say. I might have agreed with that statement had it not been for my sister showing me what happens when a family member acts as a loyal supporter despite knowing a person's every weakness and fault.

You see, in grade school I was a mess. I had a bad bowl cut. Too many freckles covered my nose. I wore the same awful navy-blue sweater every single day until it practically disintegrated. My hair held the unbecoming shine of ultraquick showers minus the shampoo. I had the worst-smelling feet. I gained a lot of weight the summer before middle school and got stretch marks. I was ashamed. While my parents worked, my sister took me to the neighborhood pool. She never said a word about my body. She only said, "I love your bathing suit." I remember. It meant everything that she chose to look beyond the unsightly marks.

In high school Rebecca would wave me over as I walked down the halls. She would introduce her awkward freshman sister to her senior-high friends. She was proud of who I was. She believed in me. My sister never told me I was not capable even if she thought there was no way I could make the volleyball team or move up a chair in orchestra. As an adult, Rebecca showed me the same support. Knowing how much I loved to write, she was adamant that I should start a blog. I said I didn't know how. She sent me a book telling me how. She said she would help. My sister kept saying I should and I could until I finally tried. I would not be a published author today had it not been for the unconditional love and encouragement I received from my sister. My life would have turned out differently if my sister had chosen to be my adversary rather than my ally.

My greatest hope is that my daughters will encourage each other this way if for no other reason than to have someone who will believe in them no matter what. In a culture where tearing down is not only accepted but encouraged ... where folks are constantly trying to "one up" each other ... where public shaming is commonplace, even among family members ... where people feel they have the right to personally attack someone if they say it through a screen ... where authority figures use condemnation to "motivate" someone to run faster or try harder, we need all the support we can get. Our society has lost its boundaries—boundaries that guide us in humane and compassionate treatment of one another. And I believe it begins at home.

Talking to Natalie about how I expect her to treat her little sister shined an uncomfortable spotlight onto my own words and actions. It is obvious that the way I used to speak to her has influenced her behavior. I cannot change the past, but I *can* do something to positively impact today and even the future. The truth is, the way I treat Natalie will reflect how she treats Avery. Just as she is shaping her little sister's self-esteem through words and actions, I am shaping hers.

> Just as I told her to think about the voice she is using with her sister—Is it kind? Is it patient? Is it encouraging? I must consider my tone too.
>
> Just as I told her to think about the messages she is giving—*You matter. You're smart. I believe in you.* I must think about my words too.
>
> Just as I told Natalie if she doesn't like Avery wearing grubby

T-shirts every day, compliment her when she wears
something you *do* like. I am trying to practice that too.
Just as I told her to notice when her sister is stressed out or
struggling and to say, "How can I help?" instead of "Just
deal with it." I must remember this too.

Those are things my big sister Rebecca did for me — not perfectly, but consistently. And it made a life-changing difference.

Shortly after my discussion with Natalie, the girls began riding
the bus to a new school. It was the first time they'd ever been
"bus riders" since our former neighborhood didn't have school
buses. On the second night of school I heard the girls talking in
the basement.

"When the teacher says walk to the bus, you need to go as fast
as you can, okay? I was worried you were going to miss it. I kept
praying you were coming. Walk real fast tomorrow. I know you
can do it," said the big sister.

"Okay, I will," promised the little sister. "Thanks for letting
nothing bad happen to me."

"I won't," said her protector.

There are boundary lines within our lives that we cannot see,
but they are powerful; they are healing; they are protective; they
are life-giving. The boundaries created in the home not only
impact how the members of our family treat each other, but also
how they treat friends, teachers, coaches, teammates, employers,
coworkers, spouses, and even people they disagree with on the
Internet. In today's culture, we need someone in our corner ...
to have our back ... to believe in us when we don't believe in
ourselves. We can do that for each other. We can do that for the
people who are learning how to treat others by watching us live.
Let us create boundaries that build up, not tear down. Let us be
role models, not bad examples. Let us leave legacies, not scars on
our sisters and brothers.

HANDS FREE LIFE DAILY DECLARATION

Today I want you to remember my listening face—not my fake listening face, the one that nods robotically and looks right through you. I want to love you by listening, really listening. Today I want you to remember my open hands—not my multitasking hands, the ones too full, too busy, too pushy to gently tuck your hair behind your ear. I want to love you by opening my two free hands. Today I want you to remember my loving voice—not my impatient, exasperated, not-right-now voice. I want to love you by speaking kindly. Today I want to remember that when I extend compassion, softness, and kindness to you, it has the potential to create a positive ripple effect touching each member of our family and every person you encounter.

ESTABLISH BOUNDARIES TO PROTECT MOMENTS

"Name twenty things you love about me," Avery requested just as I was shutting the door to her bedroom. Because I immediately thought about the dirty dishes in the sink, the work I had yet to do before I could go to bed, and the ache in my back, I almost said, "Not tonight."

But I didn't.

Instead I slowly made my way back to her bed and rattled off things like, "I love your smile ... I love the way you sing ... I love how you help your friends ... I love the way you make me laugh ... I love the way you take your time ... I love your strong hugs ..."

I made it to twenty quite quickly, and I watched the smile on Avery's face get a little bigger with each one.

"Thank you, Mama. I love how you love me," she offered back as she rolled over preparing to sleep.

It took less than one minute, this little request of hers—but

163

there is a good chance she will remember this list, this very important list.

I don't always get it right. I don't. But in the time I've spent on this Hands Free journey, my eyes have been opened. I can now see clearly that my days are made up of a million little choices—choices to grasp what really matters or let them slip through my multitasking little fingers.

That night I got it right.

I chose the girl who still stands on her tiptoes to reach the sink.
I chose the girl who still likes me to read bedtime stories to
    her and hold her hand in the parking lot.
I chose the girl who sings made-up songs while offering me
    dandelion bouquets.
I chose the girl who has wiggly teeth and a contagious laugh.

With the kitchen in disarray and deadlines looming, I chose my child. And that fact gives me great hope. In fact, whenever I am in a state of overwhelm, I revisit the twenty-question experience. It took less than one minute, but the memory could possibly last a lifetime.

When blog readers write to me describing their current state of overwhelm and ask if it's even possible for them to live Hands Free, I share the twenty-question experience. After all, there's always going to be a lot to "get done," and if we wait until life is calm or the house is clean or the work is accomplished, we will never have time to grasp the moments that matter. Oftentimes, just the stress of everyday life feels like too much. Then throw in a family crisis, a health scare, a divorce, a death, or a job loss, and the stress can seem paralyzing. Even happy events can add to the stress—a marriage, a graduation, a retirement, or a promotion also creates feelings of overwhelm. Stopping to take time for what really matters seems like the last thing anyone wants to do during those intense periods. But actually those are *precisely* the times when we most *need* to take a few minutes for the "twenty-question requests" because they have the power to steady our rapidly beating hearts and sooth our frenzied souls. We are more likely to stop for these moments when we have established boundaries that guide our hearts and protect our time. Even in periods of uncertainty and overwhelm, boundaries help us in knowing exactly what to do to protect what matters most.

That is exactly what I experienced on the Wednesday after my first book was released. I was a complete stress ball knowing *The New York Times* bestseller list would be announced to publishers that day based on a variety of factors from the previous week. Although I knew making this highly coveted list as a first-time author was highly unlikely, I couldn't turn off the flutter of hope that danced in the pit of my stomach all day.

By three o'clock I still hadn't gotten the call, and it was time to pick up my daughters from school. As I waited for them to emerge, I did what I always did at three p.m.: I silenced the notifications on my phone to protect family time. My finger hesitated briefly as I dreamed of getting that call, but I proceeded in sliding it to the Off position as usual.

Natalie had plans with her friend Catherine for the afternoon, so Avery and I enjoyed an outing by ourselves. For three blissful hours, we visited the park, grabbed some dinner, and shopped for a dress for Avery to wear to my local book signing.

While standing in the checkout line, I rummaged around in my purse to see what time it was on my phone. Much to my surprise, there were six text messages and four missed calls. I could see a partial text where three letters, *NYT*, jumped out at me. I wanted to read the entire text, but instead I put the phone back in my bag. With a trembling voice, I told Avery we must go outside and find a quiet place away from people.

My daughter could see the tears in my eyes. "What is it, Mama?" she asked with concern.

Not wanting her to be scared, I reassured her. "It's good news—it's so, so good. But I want to read it together."

Soon Avery and I stood huddled together on the sidewalk in front of the store. As a chilly night wind blew the hair back from our faces, I read the message from my marketing director out loud: "Congratulations, Rachel! You made the NYT Bestseller List!"

I bowed my head and cried.

"Mama, your book is one of the best books! Out of like … one thousand books … your book is one that people really like to read!" Avery's precious interpretation of the exciting news made the moment even sweeter. Unexpectedly, I picked her up just as I did when she was a toddler. I swirled her round and round while reciting a prayer of gratitude to God. The blissful look on Avery's face indicated she would remember this moment her whole life.

And that's when it hit me. I was smack dab in the middle of creating a sacred memory that would be filed away in Avery's mind for perhaps seventy-five years. And this moment was ours and ours alone because of the protective barriers that were in place to grasp what mattered most, even in times of overwhelm and uncertainty.

The conscientious, type-A part of me considered calling back the members of my publishing team or at least calling Scott, my parents, or my sister to share the news. But I didn't. Instead, I offered my hand to my daughter, and we chatted throughout the drive home.

I chose the girl who still gives me love notes.
I chose the girl who still finds comfort in her mother's kisses when she falls and hurts herself.
I chose the girl who says, "This dinner tastes so good," even when it's simple chicken and broccoli spears.
I chose the girl who types stories on the computer and says, "I'm a writer too, Mama."

With a full voice mail in-box and a desire to share my news with the world, I chose my child … because she was there waiting, wanting, delighting in being chosen. And this moment was meant to be ours and ours alone.

A few hours later, I finally called my literary agent, Sandra. She said, "We were worried! No one could get ahold of you."

"I was with Avery. Being Hands Free," I explained, nearly crying as the words left my lips.

I don't always get it right. I don't. And sometimes life circumstances make it even harder. But that night I made the right choice, and that gives me hope. May that hope be yours the next time you're faced with life's questions. Whether it's one big question or twenty little ones, may you have the ability to know which ones are worthy of your attention as you turn away from the noise of the world to respond to what matters most.

HANDS FREE LIFE DAILY DECLARATION

Today I might have too many things on my plate, but I will remember I don't have to do them all. Today I might have too many balls in the air, but I will remember to hold the most important ones. Today might be one mad dash from morning to night, but I will remember there is always time for hugs and kisses. Today I may have a hard time seeing the goodness through the chaos and the clutter, but I will remember to keep looking. The moments that make life worth living are found in the most unsuspecting places, in the most challenging times, if I make it a daily practice to choose what matters over what doesn't.

HANDS FREE LIFE HABIT BUILDER 7

Establish Boundaries with Hands Free House Rules

In our house, we speak kindly and respectfully even if we disagree.
In our house, human beings take precedence over electronic devices.
In our house, today matters more than yesterday.
In our house, we set out to encourage one person each day.

In our house, we look for the blessings. (When they're not obvious, we keep looking.)

In our house, we have screen-free time so we can hold pets, people, and creative passions in our hands.

In our house, we *XO Before We Go*, even if our hands are sticky, even if we're running late, even if we had cross words.

In our house, we look into each other's eyes when we speak.

In our house, we open our door and say, "Come as you are."

In our house, there's time for "one more" — one more hug, one more cleansing breath, one more prayer, and one more page of our favorite book.

In our house, grace is served daily. We're all learning here.

In our house, we love each other as is.

In our house, there's nothing wrong with doing nothing every now and then.

In our house, we put living, laughing, and loving at the top of the priority list.

In our house, there is room for mistakes and room to breathe.

As a teacher, I discovered that creating a classroom environment in which children could prosper and thrive was directly related to the rules we developed as a class and how they were articulated and modeled. Like my students, the members of my family freely add their input regarding our house rules, and we know that rules might need to be modified as we grow and change. Before you go any further on your Hands Free journey, take some time to think about what rules or boundaries might help you or your family live better and love more in the precious hours of your days. Write these ideas down and discuss them with the people you love.

Habit 8:

LEAVE A LEGACY

← ❤ ❤ ❤ →

*Carve your name on hearts, not tombstones. A legacy is etched
into the minds of others and the stories they share about you.*
                                            Shannon L. Alder

IT SEEMS ODD TO say that Avery and I walked to a graveyard every
day for an entire summer although we knew no one buried there.
What seems even more odd is that I continued to go there after
she went to school that fall. When I should've been putting myself
out there to become part of the community in which we'd moved,
I chose to sit by myself with those who'd already lived out their
earthly days.

The pull I felt to this cemetery could only be explained providentially. For most of my life, graveyards made me feel uneasy
and sad. But as soon as the moving boxes were unpacked, I felt an
unsettling in my soul. I needed to find a walking route. I needed
a place where my legs could grow tired as my spirit came alive,
just like I had in all the other places I'd lived. I never would have
guessed I would be drawn to a graveyard.

The first time I exited my subdivision on foot, the heavily
traveled roadway in front of me felt faster and more dangerous

than it ever had in the car. But I refused to be intimidated. I took a deep breath and forged ahead, hugging the outer edge of the sidewalk farthest from the busy road. With every Nissan and Chevrolet that barreled past, my hair blew back from my face and hot air hugged my legs. I kept my head down and walked briskly, pausing briefly to notice a historic cemetery on my right. I'm pretty sure I would have felt slightly creeped out if I hadn't been so focused on finding a peaceful place to walk.

Once I got past the cemetery, I saw exactly what I was looking for: an established neighborhood canopied by lush trees with no moving vehicle in sight. I immediately turned right and walked the shady maze of side streets and cul-de-sacs for an hour. When it was time to return home, I resisted the urge to walk past the cemetery at a quickened pace. Instead, I noted the names and dates of those who had lived over a century ago. Little did I know this would become my daily ritual.

Each day I laced up my running shoes pretending I might try a new route. At the exit of my subdivision, I'd stop for a moment and contemplate my choices. I knew I could turn left and then take another quick left or a right. I knew I could even go straight. But in the end, I'd always turn right. Up ahead, I could see the flags of the cemetery beckoning me forth. It brought me comfort to know exactly what three last names would be the first to greet me. Barnes, Brooks, and Settle were always there, waiting like faithful supporters along a race route. This familiarity assured my directionally challenged self that I was not lost. *The tree-covered neighborhood where you like to walk is coming up*, the tombstones would whisper. *You've been here before*, they'd say.

For some reason I decided not to give myself a hard time about this severe lack of adventure on my walking route. After all, I was learning something new practically every day. I learned new grocery store aisles and post office locations. I learned new state procedures like emission checks and school immunization requirements. I learned that people drive faster and speak more sharply here. I learned there are stoplights on the interstate, and I can be ticketed if I proceed before it is my turn to merge. I learned where light switches and thermostats are located along dark hallways. I learned names of neighbors, their children, and their pets. Moving to a new place meant my brain was constantly learning new things all day long. So when I had the opportunity to take a walk, I'd go where my feet led me: a right turn out of the neighborhood onto the familiar sidewalk that ran along the bustling thoroughfare and past the cemetery to the shaded sanctuary. It is where I walked the same loop over and over, jotting my thoughts in my tiny notebook the way I did before I moved. On one of the visits, I thought to look at the name of the peaceful street that sheltered me from the noisy rush. It was called Gracewoods. That was not a coincidence to me.

The tombstones I walked by each day had been there for a hundred years. Although I did not know anyone buried there, other people did. They would come and leave flowers and stuffed animals. They would come and simply sit in their car, too feeble or too sad to get out and kneel. But regardless of whether they kneeled or sat, brought flowers or came empty-handed, they would come and remember. They'd remember the way she hugged and didn't let go first. They'd remember the way she laughed at bad jokes just to make the joke-teller feel good. They'd remember how he claimed a daily bowl of oatmeal grew hair on your chest and that hot dogs were the best bait for catching catfish. The people who came to remember went home and did these things too. They hugged long, laughed hard, and fished with hot dogs because it made their dearly departed feel near.

Each time I walked by Brooks, Barns, and Settle, I took a moment to imagine what rituals, habits, and words live on *right now* in those who loved them. As the traffic blew by me, adamantly refusing to slow down for a nameless pedestrian, those thoughts brought great comfort—because nowadays there is little permanence. Messages disappear with the push of a button ... handwritten notes are obsolete ... sustained eye contact is a rarity. I seldom see lipstick marks on people's cheeks anymore. But that quiet graveyard flanked by a stream of busy people going to important places offered me hope. I was reminded of the power within loving rituals. Through loving daily practices, we are able to create the kind of permanence that becomes the cornerstone of a life, a GPS for a world in which we are so easily lost.

When I was especially overwhelmed or confused, I would stop and sit on the bench that Avery deemed the "shadiest" spot in the cemetery during the hottest part of the summer. There I would sit in peaceful silence, feeling myself become more centered and more optimistic with each passing minute. Without fail, I would replay something Avery had said on our second visit to the grave-yard. We'd been talking about cremation and burial and how it would be painful to see someone she loved pass away before she did. Sitting up straight on the handcrafted bench next to a family of tombs, Avery made a declaration. "When I have a friend who dies, I will come here every year on her birthday. I will come each year on my birthday. I will remember the funny things she said and did and then I will pray."

Oh yes. I hope so, my love. I hope that is exactly what you do. May you always walk against the busy traffic of life and find a shady spot to remember what matters most. May your life become a series of such meaningful rituals that live beyond your earthly days.

Suddenly, it all made sense—why this particular place at this particular juncture of my life had become my resting place ... my holy ground ... my cornerstone. Nowhere else could all my senses be simultaneously reminded of why I wanted to live Hands Free. Through faded bouquets that lay beneath dates and dash marks etched in stone, my Hands Free aspirations were confirmed. I wanted to leave the earth better than it was before; I wanted to live on in the habits, words, and memories of those who had loved and learned from me.

Leave a Legacy, the eighth intentional habit of a Hands Free Life, is about making choices to become a living, breathing example of life well lived using meaningful measures of success. By recognizing the way you want to spend your time on earth, you are better equipped to find your unique path toward a sense of fulfillment regardless of societal opinion. Through this deep connection to your soul's greatest needs and hopes, you are able to feel God's internal confirmation spurring you on. As your loved ones begin following in your footsteps to seek real-life moments and authentic connections, your efforts will be rewarded tenfold.

In this chapter, we'll explore three ways to become a living example of a Hands Free Life. Showing others that life is best lived with open hands, open eyes, and an open heart is an everlasting gift to others, as well as yourself. The best news is that the results of leaving a legacy become evident far sooner than you might expect. May you find, as I have, that you don't have to wait until your dying breath to see that your loving actions have made a difference. In the facial expressions and everyday actions of those you love, may you see your Hands Free way of life take hold. Watch as their lives become richer and their hearts become fuller as they follow your footsteps toward home.

LEAVE A LEGACY TO GRASP SIMPLE JOYS

Taking Natalie and Avery to the Indiana State Fair was one of my grand attempts to expose them to a simpler, slower way of life. I wanted to immerse them in the sights, sounds, and tastes of my childhood—the one with fresh sweet corn, glowing fireflies in Mason jars, and neighbors smiling through the front-porch screen. Little did I know this well-intentioned adventure would intensify a very uncomfortable feeling—a feeling of deep uncertainty that produced questions with no easy answers.

It happened while watching the 4-H kids show their beautifully groomed llamas. Natalie kept inching forward until she was practically part of the demonstration. For fifteen minutes she stood there unaware of anything but llama fur and 4-H badges. "I would love to live on a farm and take care of an animal like that," she dreamily confessed as we walked away from the barn to see other fair exhibits. That's precisely when I got *that feeling*.

A few minutes later, we stopped in the pioneer village and

watched a woman in historical garb demonstrate how to churn butter. For nearly ten minutes Avery was her number-one fan. Avery intently studied the woman's skillful hands as they worked their magic. Just one taste of the creamy concoction convinced Avery that we must never buy store-bought butter ever again. When she insisted that we start making our own butter, I got *that feeling* again.

That uncomfortable feeling of uncertainty and doubt that flared at the state fair was not new. In fact, every time I read about families selling virtually all of their material possessions to drastically downsize, I felt it. Every time I read about folks growing their own produce, eating only real food, and composting their garbage, I felt it. And every time I visited the outdoor section of Home Depot and longed for a job with flowers, seeds, and sunshine, I felt it. It was that feeling that said: *Am I doing this all wrong? Could there be more to life (or perhaps I should say less) than the way I am currently living it?*

I believe it is perfectly normal to consider other ways of life and the benefits of varying approaches. In fact, I find myself doing it quite often on this Hands Free journey. But as I began to notice the stark contrast between my childhood and the one my children were experiencing, I felt an unhealthy panic that I was doing it "wrong." As I watched the world become more digitized and more commercialized ... more processed, more public, and more pressured ... more frantic and more frenzied, I couldn't help but wonder if I should make major changes in my family's eating, sleeping, and living habits. But before I banned all Apple products from our home and exchanged my car for a secondhand llama, I discovered that drastic measures are not required to grasp the simple joys of life—just some heightened awareness and some new experiences.

I was having one of my *Is-There-a-Better-Way-of-Life?* daydreaming sessions in the outdoor garden section of Home Depot. While standing next to a display of brilliant orange mums, I paused for a moment to feel the sun on my face. I could hear my daughters' voices drifting through the fall breeze. As they considered cacti or pepper plants for the back porch, my favorite quote of all time came flooding back to me.

> Do not ask your children
> to strive for extraordinary lives.
> Such striving may seem admirable,
> but it is the way of foolishness.
> Help them instead to find the wonder
> and the marvel of an ordinary life.
> Show them the joy of tasting
> tomatoes, apples and pears.
> Show them how to cry
> when pets and people die.
> Show them the infinite pleasure
> in the touch of a hand.
> And make the ordinary come alive for them.
> The extraordinary will take care of itself.
>
> William Martin*

In a matter of minutes, I felt more hopeful than I had in months about the way I was living. The part about tasting fruit and crying when pets die was the clincher. I can do this! I thought to myself with clarity. I have the ability to make the ordinary come alive right here in my current life. And perhaps it doesn't require a move to the country, raising farm animals in the backyard, or selling my entire shoe collection to make it happen.

But ... I had to be realistic. Making the ordinary come alive would require time and effort. I knew all too well that my "stuff" had the tendency to take over and cover up what was truly important. In my home, in my daily schedule, and in the essence of my very being, life had the potential to become a continuous cycle of scrolling, clicking, completing, purchasing, committing,

---

* William Martin, "Make the Ordinary Come Alive," *The Parent's Tao Te Ching: Ancient Advice for Modern Parents* (Cambridge, Mass.: Da Capo, 1999), 59. Used with permission.

shuttling, competing, rushing, consuming, pressuring, uploading, posting, and primping. Those were the very behaviors that nearly cost me everything I held dear when I was living distracted.

Yet as my daughters discussed which homegrown herbs would be safe for our cat when it was on the porch, I was inspired. I vowed to make it a daily practice to seek out at least one simple joy in an ordinary day. In the week that followed, I discovered that grasping meaningful moments came more easily than I ever thought possible. With heightened awareness, we caught a glimpse of the extraordinary in the midst of the ordinary by:

- hopping on our bikes after dinner for a quick ride and pointing to a "cotton candy" sky
- staying just five extra minutes at bedtime to hear things on my child's heart that seem to only come out in the darkness
- watching the antics of Banjo the cat while the homework waited a few minutes to be completed
- holding Natalie's hand as we walked into swim-team practice and thinking how good it felt
- going to the farmer's market on Saturday morning and trying every apple there was to sample and conveniently forgetting that we left the house a mess
- working side by side with my children to remove unused items from their bedrooms and donating the extra clothes and extra toys to families who would use and enjoy them
- asking pet owners if my daughters and I could pet their dogs as they walked by and watching their faces when they talked about their beloved companion
- stopping to admire the way a street vendor used a Coke bottle for a flower vase and using that example to talk about the meaning of repurposing

Those are a few examples of how our family noticed and savored the simple joys without a lot of extra effort, cost, or inconvenience. The best part, though, was how these intentional actions inspired further actions in my children. Natalie made lip gloss out of old crayons and Vaseline — her version of repurposing. She also began packing tiny apples from the farmer's market for snack rather than boxed crackers. Avery spent an entire Saturday morning clearing the clutter from the top of her dresser. She changed the focal point of her desk from material possessions to a living being — a fish named Violet, which she fed daily and watched with delight. Both children delighted in contributing fresh red peppers to our dinner salad that were grown in their miniature gardens on the porch.

It's definitely not minimalist living, but it's less. It's not raising livestock, but it's caring for God's creatures. It's not the experience of a farmhand, but it's a taste of homegrown. These small acts of meaningful living showed me that I have more influence on my family than I previously thought. There is hope for those growing up in a drive-through, task-oriented, materialistic, and competition-driven society. That hope is in my hands.

If I want my children to be awed by sunsets, I must take time to be awed by extraordinary sights in nature.

If I want my children to appreciate the softness of a beautiful animal, I must take time to appreciate soft, cuddly creatures.

If I want my children to relish in the joys of a screen-free Saturday, I must express joy in going off the grid.

If I want my children to value experiences rather than things, I must celebrate a spontaneous run through the sprinkler, good conversation, snowball fights, and crickets that lull us to sleep.

If I want my children to experience the freedom that comes from open blue skies and crunchy leaves underfoot, I must partake in such freedoms myself.

If I want my children to look straight into the eyes of those who speak to them, I must look into their eyes and listen to their words.

If I want my children to seek real-life moments and real-life
connections now and in the future, I must live by example.

I can't expect the world to show them life is best lived with
open hands, open eyes, and an open heart. It must come from
me. There must be sacred pauses in our daily schedule so there
is time to notice the everyday miracles around us. Thankfully,
drastic life changes are not necessary to do this. It is possible
to incorporate elements of a simpler, slower, more natural, and
more gratitude-filled life into my current one. The hope is in my
hands, and I have the power to offer it to my children and future
grandchildren.

Although I didn't think my newfound hope for grasping life's
simple joys needed further solidifying, God offered one final confirmation to seal it. Our family had driven to a new park in our
city where we'd enjoyed a picnic and played on the swings. We
were packing up our things when I noticed a well-tended war
memorial behind the picnic pavilion.

"Let's check out the memorial before we go," I suggested,
pointing to a marble wall surrounded by two majestic flags and
blooming rosebushes.

Our family spent a few minutes reading the brick walkway
that bore the names of those who'd made the ultimate sacrifice
for our country. Avery was especially interested and asked me to
read all the names while Natalie proceeded to walk to the car
with Scott. After patiently waiting for several minutes, Natalie
hollered, "Time to go!" But my small, freckle-faced Noticer had
her eyes fixed on one particular memorial brick. Natalie's sum-
mons did not stir Avery. She didn't even look up. I remained silent
and waited.

Avery crouched down and gathered a handful of fallen rose
petals from the blooming bushes. She took the loose petals and
walked them over to the brick of an army specialist and placed them
carefully round his name. Then she scattered a few more beneath
the flagpole. After standing back as if to admire the improved look
of the memorial, she stated, "I'm ready now, Mama."

In one heartfelt gesture, my child solidified the way I believe God wants me to live out my twenty-first-century life. I wrote it down so I could refer to it whenever that feeling of uncertainty and doubt flared up:

If you should happen to catch a glimpse of what really matters in life, regard it with care. Decorate it with flowers. Cover it with love. Hold it in the sunshine. Give it a little bit of time and attention. And when the world tries to push you forward, listen to your heart instead. Because if *you* don't make time for what really matters, no one is going to do it for you. Taking a few minutes to savor everyday wonders makes the heart fuller, the inner doubts quieter, and the human connections stronger. And that's when the ordinary becomes extraordinary for yourself and those who share your life. (No drastic measures or pet llamas necessary.)

 ## HANDS FREE LIFE DAILY DECLARATION

I want my loved ones to spend less time on digital devices. I want them to see beyond the electronic screen. I want them to know what life feels like in their hands, not through a keyboard. I want to ensure that the people in my life have the capacity to connect to humans, nature, and life in the real world. I will lead by example. I will be their guide for finding simple joy in the everyday routines of life. This may mean setting limits on tech time, extending invitations for nonmedia activities, and taking substantial breaks from the online world. At times leading by example may feel uncomfortable, inconvenient, unpopular, and ineffective. But each time I see the people I love holding what really matters in their mitten-clad or dirt-caked hands, I will be reminded of how important this gift truly is now and in their future.

LEAVE A LEGACY TO INSPIRE A FUTURE GENERATION

The morning rush typical of most downtown coffee shops had died down. I didn't have to strain to hear the words of the beautiful twentysomething writer with bright, clear eyes sitting across from me. Her fingers were perched above something that resembled an iPad. She was ready to take notes for a magazine article she was writing about my journey.

Would she get it? I wondered. Would she understand the relevance of the Hands Free message or would she think that I am out of touch with what is important in the modern world?

The writer interrupted my insecure thoughts with a warm and welcoming offer: "Instead of asking questions, I like to ask people just to tell their stories. I find they don't leave anything out that way."

Tell me your story. I was suddenly hopeful. This sounded like the start of the best interview I'd ever had.

I was no more than five minutes in when I told the most important part of my story: the kiss that my then-four-year-old daughter had placed on the palm of my hand. It happened when I took my first step to be less distracted and more present. I'd temporarily let go of all my distractions—the phone, computer, to-do list ... the pressure, perfection, guilt—and simply held Avery. Her response was a kiss on my hand that ultimately changed my life.

The young woman's fingers stopped typing. Her eyes had that unmistakable shine of unspilled tears. She blinked in rapid succession as if trying to force the emotion from escaping. "Wow" was all she said.

"It's very emotional," I agreed, feeling moved by her heartfelt reaction.

I continued, describing more experiences like the kiss that kept propelling me forward on my journey toward a less distracted, more meaningfully connected life.

"As you are talking, I keep thinking of my favorite quote," the young lady said, cupping her steaming coffee with one free hand.

" 'If nobody speaks of remarkable things, how can they be called remarkable?' " she recited. "It's from a book by Jon McGregor. I loved the quote so much that I painted the words on a canvas and hung it in my apartment." Her face lit up as she divulged this little bit about herself—this bit that revealed what made her heart sing.

It was my turn to be captivated. I felt as if she had just given me a gift—a gift of understanding ... of unity ... of camaraderie. This beautiful young lady got *exactly* what I was saying—she recognized the importance of living with open hands and open eyes. Like Avery, she was a Noticer of remarkable things. I vowed not to forget her beautiful offering. Little did I know just how much it would impact me in the hours ahead.

After leaving the coffee shop, I headed to my daughters' school. I had been invited to speak to a second-grade Girl Scout troop about achieving their dreams. I'd jotted some notes, a few things I wanted to be sure to tell the children about setting goals and using positive affirmations.

But as the girls sat in front of me like little sponges with expectant eyes, I felt compelled to share specifics from my personal journey rather than offer vague generalizations. But would they get it? Or would the story of my highly distracted life sound like a foreign language to them? Would they stare at the clock wondering how many agonizing minutes until my talk was over?

Despite my reservations, I told my story. And when I got to the part about Avery's kiss on my hand, there were a few little gasps ... a few smiles ... a few shining eyes.

I looked around carefully to make sure everyone was still with me. Even my own daughters, who sat at a table in the back of the room, looked at me with hopeful faces, wanting to hear the story they'd heard many times before.

And so I continued. I told the children how I wrote about the kiss on the hand and published it on a blog. I told them how my story inspired other people to look for their own *Kiss on the Hand* moments—those beautiful moments we so often miss in our busy, distracted lives. I told the girls about how I kept publishing weekly blog posts for years until finally a book publisher took notice and thought my story was worthy of printing.

I held up my finished book, my 240 pages of little moments that made life worth living. And when I did, I saw fire in those children's eyes. I saw dreams igniting right then and there.

"Tell me your dreams," I said. "What do you hope to accomplish?"

One by one, their small hands raised triumphantly.

"Veterinarian."

"Singer on *The Voice*."

"Pro basketball player."

"College softball player."

"Robot inventor."

"Olympic ice skater."

"Teacher."

"Published author."

"But what if someone says, 'You can't do that'? What if someone says, 'You don't have a chance'? What if someone says, 'You're no good'?" I challenged.

"Don't listen to them!" one girl fired back.

"You know what you should listen to?" I asked. "Listen to your heart when you hold that basketball. Listen to your heart when you take that pencil in your hand and can't stop writing. Think about what it feels like to sing at the top of your lungs. Think about what it feels like to do something you love to do. But don't stop there. Share that incredible feeling with someone else. Because if we share *our* remarkable thing, someone else might notice *his* or *her* remarkable thing."

I searched the girls' faces one by one. They were still with me—listening, learning, and digesting what I had to offer. And that's when I leaned forward and lowered my voice to almost a whisper. "Maybe you don't make it to *The Voice*. Maybe you don't make the pros or land a book deal. That doesn't mean you didn't succeed. Maybe sharing your journey, your dream, or what excites your heart *is* the achievement. Maybe inspiring someone else to see his or her life differently *is* the success."

After receiving big hugs and signing books for each precious girl, I walked out of the building with my daughters. As always, Natalie was five steps ahead. I held back for my stop-and-smell-the-roses younger child.

As I fell in stride with Avery's leisurely gait, she grabbed my hand. "I teached you, Mama? Tell me again what I teached you."

Although my children were not part of the Girl Scout troop, it was apparent this little girl had listened to my presentation and wanted to hear a certain part again. I was happy to oblige. "You taught me that life should not be lived in a hurry. You taught me that if I slowed down, I could see all the beautiful things. You always had this huge smile on your face and I didn't. That's when I realized I could learn a lot from you about living life."

Avery suddenly stopped walking and looked up, her little glasses teetering on the edge of her nose. "Remember when I kissed your hand, Mama? That's when I changed your life."

For a moment, I had no words. I was suddenly overwhelmed with gratitude for the gift I received from a twentysomething writer with hopeful eyes who let me tell my story over coffee.

If nobody speaks of remarkable things, how can they be called remarkable?

How can they spread like a kiss drifting in the wind?

How can they inspire a future generation?

How can they find their way back to the person who created one of the most remarkable moments of your life?

Now, more than ever, we must speak of remarkable things. Now, when undivided attention is a rare and priceless commodity ... now, when we too often choose glowing screens over shining sunlight ... now, when digital notifications take precedence over soul-to-soul connection.

Now more than ever, we must speak of the remarkable things that make our heart sing ... that fill our eyes with tears ... that bring beauty, comfort, and joy to our ordinary, mundane lives.

You may think the person on the other end won't get it.

But maybe she will.

So speak. Speak of what makes your heart sing. Speak of what alters the way you see your life.

Because you never know who might be listening . . .

And using your dream to envision her own.

HANDS FREE LIFE DAILY DECLARATION

Today I will vocalize my dreams. Maybe it is to run a race . . . to dance . . . to go back to school . . . to create art and sell my wares . . . to write . . . to reveal something beautiful inside me that the world needs to see. I might get discouraged. I might be misunderstood. I might feel scared. But I vow to remember that in taking this risk, there might just be "successes" unimagined. Maybe I will inspire someone else. Maybe I will experience happiness. Maybe my children will make a bold move because I did. Maybe my heart will sing in a way I never knew it could.

LEAVE A LEGACY OF SELF-KINDNESS

It was a simple enough recipe—place peanuts and several types of chocolate in a Crock-Pot for two hours and then scoop out the melted mixture in dollops to create bite-size treats. Simple, right? Well, not if you forget about it for four hours.

Avery came downstairs when she smelled a pungent odor wafting from the kitchen. "What is that horrible smell, Mama?" she asked, scrunching up her face as I scraped peanuts that now resembled black beans into the sink.

"Oh, I just wasted four bags of chocolate chips because I forgot to turn off the Crock-Pot. I cannot believe I did that!" I chastised myself as I aggressively shoved charred clumps of chocolate into the garbage disposal. "And now I don't have anything to bring to the party." I didn't try to hide my disappointment. I just couldn't believe I'd messed up something so simple.

That's when a little voice of wisdom cut right through the burned haze of my frustration. "Everybody makes mistakes, remember?" she reminded me. "Be nice to yourself," instructed my curly haired daughter.

Those had been *my* words to her over the past few years. But it hadn't always been that way. During my distracted years, minor kid mishaps and trivial mistakes were viewed as major inconveniences that derailed my perfectly orchestrated plans. But living with a mother who lost it over spilled cereal and broken eyeglasses was not the life I wanted for my children. After witnessing the fear in Natalie's eyes when she spilled a bag of rice, I prayed for the strength and patience to look beyond the mess and mayhem. In my children's openly flawed existence and endearing little quirks, God showed me something worthy of love and forgiveness. I began offering my children love without condition and restraint, and when I did, their little faces glowed with validation and acceptance. To love someone *as is* was a gift, I realized.

Whenever Natalie and Avery messed up, I learned to say, "Be kind to yourself. Everyone makes mistakes." As my children grew, they began saying it to themselves and to each other. And one day, while berating myself over a burned Crock-Pot and ruined recipe, those words came back to me. And for the first time in my life, I believed they really did apply to me too.

I decided that multiple decades of being unkind to myself was enough. It was quite enough. *Be kind to yourself . . . only love today.* I began saying these words. Sometimes ten thousand times a day, I said them.

Only love today. Only love today. Be kind to yourself. Be kind to yourself. This healing mantra became a song on repeat. And it was working. These empowering words were silencing the bully in my head. There was a crack of light. I was able to see the next steps: I would stop beating myself up over past failures. I would stop replaying mistakes over and over in my head. I would be open about my shortcomings, real with my humanness, and generous with my apologies.

"I don't always get it right, and I never will," I honestly admitted to myself. But miraculously, I did not see that as failing, nor was it something to be sad about. There was a silver lining: on the days I didn't get it right, my children were still learning valuable lessons about life, persistence, determination, failure, compassion, authenticity, grace, and forgiveness. *Even when I wasn't getting it "right," it didn't mean my children were going to turn out all wrong.* My humanness allowed my children to be human. My courage to keep showing up gave my children courage to show up. Loving myself despite my failures, flaws, and imperfections gave my children permission to love themselves as is. As a result, my children discovered much sooner something I wished I'd known all my life: you can't see the silver lining that comes from falling down until you get back up.

But I see it now. I see it now. Even after forty years, it was not too late.

I must admit that I still have bad days—I do. But the tendency to go easy on myself is stronger than my tendency to bully myself. This is significant because it used to be the other way around. My knee-jerk reaction was to criticize, condemn, and not-good-enough myself to death. That was a brutal and hopeless way to live.

It's taken four years of baby steps to get to this place of loving myself as is. But it began with a single mantra: *Only love today. Be kind to yourself.* Those God-given words shut down the bully and threw me a lifeline. And when I grabbed it and pulled myself up, I saw two little girls looking on their authentically messy, hopelessly flawed mother with love in their eyes and relief in their chests. That's when I saw the silver lining. It shined so brightly that I could see every blemish, every imperfection on my tattered soul.

I couldn't have hidden them if I tried.

But I didn't want to hide anymore.

I had two very good reasons not to.

HANDS FREE LIFE DAILY DECLARATION

Today I will love myself right where I am . . . not when I lose weight . . . not when I accomplish this or that . . . not when I get my life straightened out. I will look at myself in my mess and mayhem and remember that I am a human being capable of mistakes and worthy of God's grace. I will speak words of kindness and compassion to myself even when they are not the first words that come to mind. Today I will choose to love myself because I want my children to choose to love themselves too. Loving myself may not be how I started, but it can be who I am now and how I am remembered when I am gone.

HANDS FREE LIFE HABIT BUILDER 8

Leave a Legacy with the Presence Pledge

I hope you feel like a welcomed spark to my life, not an inconvenience, annoyance, or bother to my day.

I hope you feel comfortable in your skin, not constantly wondering how many things you need to change before you're loved and celebrated.

I hope you feel heard, valued, and understood, not dismissed for being too young or too inexperienced to have an opinion or know what you need to thrive.

I hope you feel capable and confident, not incapable of trying new things without constant supervision and correction.

I hope you feel brave to bare the colors of your soul, not pressured to hide your light or play small to gain acceptance.

I hope after spending an hour . . . a day . . . a lifetime in my presence,

I leave your heart fuller,
  your smile wider,
  your spirit stronger
  your future brighter
than you could have ever imagined by yourself.

Never in my life could I remember being so profoundly impacted by a single question than I was by this one written by psychotherapist and mom Andrea Nair: "How do my children feel about themselves as a result of spending time with me?"

After reading that question, it stuck with me. Each time I was in the presence of my children, I thought about it. That question motivated me to speak more kindly and listen more intently than I ever had in the past. But it didn't stop there. Andrea's question popped into my head when I was in the company of Scott, my parents, my sister, friends, colleagues, and even grocery store workers who helped carry my groceries to the car. I soon realized that by making others feel loved and heard while in my presence, I could live the kind of legacy I'd always wanted to live—one that left the world a better place upon my departure.

Habit 9:

CHANGE SOMEONE'S STORY

←———— ❤ ❤ ————→

*The place God calls you to is the place where your deep gladness
and the world's deep hunger meet.*

Frederick Buechner

FROM THE TIME AVERY was a toddler, new situations caused
anxiety to well up inside her. And truth be told, I felt anxious
too. With each unfamiliar building, each new teacher, and every
"first" Avery faced, I'd hold my breath and gently nudge her forth.
I always hoped my assurances sounded stronger than I felt. There
was just something about this child whose glasses sat on the tip of
her nose, whose unruly hair would refuse to behave in an orderly
fashion, whose inner firefly light was only seen when someone
took time to really know her that made me want to protect her.
Avery had described herself differently from the rest enough times
for me to believe it was true. She marched to her own beat, made
up her own lyrics, and sang like no one was listening. Avery was a
friend to all but not really attached to one. I often wondered what
would come of her unique spirit in this hard, fast-paced world that
could so carelessly hurt and hinder.

Meet the Teacher Day at my daughters' new school was one

of those particular situations where I wanted to hold Avery close and shield her from worldly harm. She'd had trouble sleeping the night before due to the butterflies in her stomach and the questions that plagued her mind. *Would I be liked here? Would I be okay here? Would my teacher be nice? Would I have any friends?*

Upon walking in the front door, the difference between my children's former school and their new one was palpable. Going from knowing everyone we passed in the hall to walking amongst a thousand strangers was intimidating to say the least. Despite our reservations, my daughters and I maneuvered through the crowd. We successfully purchased their school spirit T-shirts, deposited money in their lunch accounts, and visited both classrooms. The initial meeting with Avery's teacher had gone exceptionally well. We'd sat in small chairs getting to know each other and even shared a few laughs. Avery had spied a lollipop "tree" behind the teacher's desk that delighted her. She left the room smiling her squinty-eye smile—the one where the corners of her mouth merged with the corners of her eyes. Her sunflower-on-steroids expression of joy was literally stuck on her face as we slowly made our way through the packed halls toward the exit door.

As we descended the steps with hundreds of other students who'd come to meet their teacher, I noticed a woman coming right for us. No matter how many people were in her way, she was determined to get to us. It was as if she knew us. It was as if she must reach us.

Finally this tall, slender woman with a welcoming smile stood directly in front of us. My children and I came to a halt. That's when this lovely woman leaned down and gently cupped Avery's face in her hands. In a deep, warm voice that held a hint of Southern charm, she said, "You are so cute. You are so, so cute. I just can't stand it! Who *are* you?" she asked excitedly.

Avery's eyes shifted over to me without removing her face from the woman's hands. She began giggling like this was the funniest and most wonderful thing that could possibly happen. "I'm Avery," she responded between giggles.

"Well, you are beautiful, Avery. I just love your freckles. I'm so glad you're here. I'm the P.E. teacher."

How this woman knew to pick Avery out of the crowd, I did not know. How she knew to take both my daughters under her wing and introduce them to the principal and associate principal, I did not know. As I fought back tears of relief and gratitude, I did know one thing: what was happening in that moment was incredibly significant. I just didn't yet know *how* significant.

Avery went home and reenacted the whole scene for her visiting grandparents. When Scott came home, she acted it out again, never leaving out the face—the face in the hands was the most important part. Avery called one of her friends back home. "You will never guess what happened to me today," she said, clutching the phone with a wide smile.

Suddenly the most wonderful realization occurred to me: this was Avery's story! Throughout her life, people would tell her their stories—like the day they met their spouse or the day they found a winning lottery ticket in a puddle next to their car or the day they quit their dead-end job to follow their dreams. In turn, Avery would tell her story. She would describe the day she was picked out of the crowd and held with loving hands—the moment her anxiety eased and her outlook brightened.

In the days following Avery's exchange with her P.E. teacher, there was a noticeable difference in my child. Particularly on P.E. days, Avery would hop right out of bed excitedly. "I am going to see the lady with the big smile," she'd tell me as she put on her gym shoes. "You know, the one who held my face," she'd remind me, as if I could possibly forget.

Because of the profound impact this positive interaction had on Avery, I felt compelled to share the story on my blog. Within twenty-four hours of hitting the publish button, over 100,000 people had read and shared the post. Commenters left incredibly touching stories about how one small gesture of kindness during a moment of despair had changed their view of the situation and for some, even the way they viewed the world. I sent the blog post to the P.E. teacher, Mrs. Janas, through email. It was imperative that she knew how she affected Avery and so many others. The exchange of several email messages between the two of us resulted in a divinely orchestrated meeting. Brought together were Mrs. Janas, myself, and a longtime reader of my blog who had introduced Mrs. Janas to my writing six months before my child's path crossed with this particular teacher. On a sunlit patio one August evening, the three of us gathered with our families. By the constant stream of conversation amongst us, you would have thought we'd known each other more than just a few days. The commonalities between the three families were so unbelievable that it was apparent that God brought us together for a reason.

That night, Mrs. Janas looked into my tearful eyes and told me about the ripples of goodness she experienced as a result of that initial interaction with Avery. The ripples began in her own heart and expanded with every person who read and reacted to the story. I told Mrs. Janas about people as far away as Russia, Africa, and New Zealand who'd been inspired to action after hearing Avery's story. All over the world, someone was telling a story of love, understanding, compassion, patience, and understanding. And it all began by Mrs. Jana's placing loving hands beneath the chin of a nervous child and letting her know she mattered.

In that moment it was all I could do not to fall to my knees and thank God for highlighting this final and most important piece of living Hands Free. *Changing Someone's Story* is vital to conquering worldly distraction, negativity, and fear to live freely and love fully.

From that point, I vowed to stop worrying so much about Avery's unique light being squelched out in this often cold, harsh world. Instead I would encourage her to be a Story Changer, like Mrs. Janas. I would keep praising her ability to notice those in pain and her desire to take action. I would stop worrying so much about what *could happen* to my children and instead focus on what they *could make happen*. Love, compassion, understanding are inside us all just waiting to touch a face, bring a smile, or wipe a tear from an eye. With every human story that is changed for good, there is one less story of hate, violence, greed, and animosity. With every life touched, the world becomes a better place. Rather than fretting about a cruel, selfish world, *Changing Someone's Story* became my focus. And now it can become yours.

Change Someone's Story, the ninth habit of a Hands Free Life, is about bettering the world by offering spontaneous gestures of compassion to those we may or may not know. Although it is easy to worry about how our loved ones will fare in today's violent, narcissistic, and often bleak world, we must remember there is goodness too. More importantly, we must remember that we have the power to create that goodness. By noticing the pain in the faces around us and reaching out without hesitation, we can cultivate hope where there once was none.

In this chapter, we'll reflect on how you can seize everyday opportunities to *Change Someone's Story* and produce ripples of positivity throughout society. May you discover that you need not go abroad or into dangerous territories to make a profound difference. May you find that whether your hand is small, large, wrinkled, smooth, dirty, or clean, it has the potential to create a more humane world. One simple gesture of kindness has the potential to change the entire outlook of one person, one family, one world, and then come back to the one who started it. By *Changing Someone's Story* we can transform the world one beautiful face at a time.

CHANGE SOMEONE'S STORY BY RESPONDING WITH EMPATHY

Avery is the only person I know who rejoices when she gets sick. Strep throat is her illness of choice. She never really feels bad when she has it, yet she cannot go to school until the antibiotics have been in her system for twenty-four hours. To Avery, that's a win–win situation. So there she was, on this particular day, in one of her ideal sick-but-not-too-sick scenarios. With one dose of amoxicillin down the hatch, Avery began celebrating. To no one in particular she announced that she would be having "alone time with Mom" while her "pink medicine made her stref throat un-contagious."

I accepted the fact that I would not get much work accomplished that day, but I knew from past "sick" days with Avery that I would make progress in other, more meaningful areas. This particular child has that way about her.

After making a work-related phone call that I could not postpone, Avery and I planned to go to the pet store and replace Banjo's missing identification collar. After looking at the fish in the glass tanks, we planned to go out to lunch. Avery mentioned that she would be careful not to breathe on anyone. "Remember, I'm contagious!" she exclaimed, looking a little too happy for such a condition.

As we prepared ourselves for the outing, I was reminded of one of the many reasons I love hanging out with my little Noticer. Minimal prepping is required before leaving the house because Avery looks beyond appearance. It is not that you have brushed your hair until it shines or that you have on the trendiest pair of jeans. In Avery's book, it's all about the smile you wear on your face.

As expected, Avery didn't comb her hair. Instead, she secured her mess of curls in a ponytail with a glittery band. I followed suit by forgoing the hairbrush and threw on my favorite ball cap. Avery immediately commented. "That hat looks so good on you, Mama." She read the words on the hat aloud. "Life is Good." After pondering that notion for a moment, she made a correction. "But it really should say, 'Life is *great*.' Because life *is* great!"

That's the moment I knew with certainty that I must pay attention. I knew I must push away thoughts of deadlines, laundry, bills, calories, worries, and regrets. I needed to be fully aware. I felt God's divine presence tapping me on the shoulder saying, "This outing has the potential to be something quite special if you choose to be *all there*."

After spending some time looking at fish and being fascinated by the machine that magically inscribed the word *BANJO* on a

shiny, metallic tag, we headed to Avery's favorite fast-food restaurant. While I stood in line and ordered, Avery chose a cozy
booth in the back of the restaurant. Within minutes, the server
slid our tray of food across the counter toward me. As I reached for
the tray, a young man wearing a pristine shirt adorned with the
restaurant logo stepped up beside me. With a solemn expression
he asked, "May I carry it?"

The man's tone was unfriendly and lacked emotion, but his
eyes said otherwise. I could have very well carried that tray myself,
but I felt the need to oblige, just as I would a child offering me a
flower or a handmade card. I could tell the man wanted to assist
and I should accept.

The slender young man with curly brown hair stiffly carried
our food to the table. Along the way, I asked him how his day was
going. His mechanical use of pat phrases reminded me of some of
the students I taught in special education. I pointed to the table
where Avery sat, and he set the tray down in front of her. I smiled
and thanked him. The man did not smile back; he simply nodded
and strode off to see if other customers needed assistance.

"Is he special, Mama?" my daughter asked curiously while
opening her ketchup. She'd heard so many stories about my former students with behavioral and learning difficulties over the
years that she could refer to them by name.

"Yes, he is," I acknowledged, feeling a bit surprised that she'd
picked up on his uniqueness that quickly. "His job is to carry
trays, put trash in trash cans, refill drinks, and things like that,"
I explained.

As Avery dug her spoon into the thick Oreo milkshake, she
smiled brightly, "I am glad he has that job. Out of all the jobs in
a restaurant, I think the helper job is the perfect job for him," she
said confidently.

A few minutes later the young man came back and asked if I
needed a refill on my drink. I told him I would love a refill and
what I was drinking.

"Remove the lid," he said robotically.

With short, quick strides he returned with a cup that was filled to the brim. Because it had no lid, the soda spilled when he set the cup down. A look of distress filled his eyes and his face became flushed. I grabbed my napkin before the liquid could drip onto my lap.

I was just about to say it was okay, but Avery spoke first. And her response was far better than what I was planning to say.

"That happens to me," Avery said, looking straight into the young man's face with a reassuring smile. She did not say the usual, "It's okay," or "Don't worry about it." She said, "That happens to me." Who knew such love, compassion, understanding, and human kindness could be contained in four simple words?

The waiter looked down shyly, and I detected a slight sigh of relief. When he left, Avery repeated her initial thoughts about the man. "I am glad he has that job. He's good at his job." Apparently a little spilled soda didn't make him any less of a good helper in her eyes.

A few minutes later, I carried our tray to the trash receptacle. Because Avery spent most of her time drinking the milkshake, her full glass of ice water had gone untouched. Much to my dismay, the paper cup tipped and hit the floor with a thud. As ice cubes and water spread across the floor, my eyes searched for our helpful friend. Unfortunately, he was nowhere to be found. Instead, a waitress came from behind the counter to survey the damage. She did not try to hide her displeasure.

"I'm very sorry," I said sincerely. "Luckily, it's just water," I added.

With a disapproving shake of her head, the waitress turned on her heel, most likely to fetch a mop. There I stood in the middle of what was now a pretty good-sized puddle. I suddenly felt very small and slightly embarrassed. I was back in middle school, all eyes on the one who clumsily dropped her tray on the cafeteria floor.

The side door that led to the drive-through line suddenly burst open and there appeared the young man. Oddly, he didn't even glance at the spill. Instead he looked directly into my eyes and said, "It's all good."

Call me crazy, but I'm pretty sure his restaurant training didn't include that line. Oh no, that line came straight from the heart.

"It's all good."

I looked down at my shoes, now dripping with moisture. The water had made its way around chair legs and into tile cracks. But when I looked at the way the liquid spread across the floor with absolutely no boundaries, a beautiful thought came to mind:

Compassion spreads.

Compassion is contagious.

Just a few minutes before my H_2O disaster, a little girl with uncombed hair and a milkshake mustache had offered kindness to a young man working hard at his job. When he'd made a mistake, she stepped into the mess with him by letting him know she makes mistakes too. Little did I know he would offer it back to me when I was in need of a little kindness and understanding.

"We are all just waiting for someone to notice—notice our pain, notice our scars, notice our fear, notice our joy, notice our triumphs, notice our courage. And the one who notices is a rare and beautiful gift." I'd written those words by observing the way Avery goes through life. But in that moment I knew there was even more to that theory.

The one who notices and responds with empathy can create a ripple effect. Because compassion spreads . . . compassion is contagious.

For a brief moment, I felt sad. I knew how important it was to respond with empathy, but in my daily life I often forgot the power of compassion. Among the busyness and the hurry, honest mistakes became bigger deals than they actually were. Among the daily distractions and pressures, small blunders were treated like major catastrophes. How easy it was to sigh with exasperation as if my whole day was ruined by one tiny mistake that might inconvenience my life for a whole two minutes. How easy it was to forget that I made mistakes too.

As Avery and I walked hand in hand through the restaurant parking lot, I knew why God wanted me to pay attention that day. It was so I could write the following words and try my hardest to live them each and every day I am blessed to be alive.

Let us notice each other's pain and ambivalence.

Even if we are different.

Even if we don't wear the same clothes.

Even if we don't have the same job or the same IQ.

Because in our hearts, we are more alike than we are different.

Let us acknowledge each other's slipups and failures with
    compassion and grace.

Even if it does cause a mess.

Even if it takes a moment of our time.

Even if it's the last thing we feel like doing.

*Because in our eyes, we are all just looking for someone to stand
    beside us in our mess.*

Let us respond with patience to the mistakes of our children.

Even if we've never made such a mistake.

Even if we saw it coming.

Even if we are at our wit's end.

*Because in our memory banks, we can all remember standing in the
    school cafeteria with the eyes of judgment on us.*

Let us notice when someone is struggling to get it right, fit
    in, or please.

Even if it's not perfect.

Even if his hands shake.

Even if someone else does it far better.

Because in our souls, we are all hungry for acceptance.

Each day when I wake up, I strive to take a page from Avery's book. I look in the mirror and say, "I will spend minimal time on my hair and put more energy into my smile. And all mistakes will be met with, 'That happens to me too.'"

Call me crazy, but I truly believe that those three aspirations have the potential to make life go from good to great—or at least cure what ails you in heart, mind, body, and soul.

HANDS FREE LIFE DAILY DECLARATION

Today when someone messes up, I will not keep track. Today when someone spills, I will not let out an exasperated sigh. Today I will meet blunders with "Everybody makes mistakes" or "That happens to me." Today I will take a page from the book of kindness and compassion. Today I will be the Giver of Second Chances, the Giver of Hugs, the Giver of Grace not just for those in my path but also for myself. And something tells me that my day will be better because of it.

CHANGE SOMEONE'S STORY BY OPENING YOUR ARMS

I carry little notebooks with me when I take walks because that's when my best writing ideas come to life. They usually start with just a few words. Sometimes those words become a poem. Sometimes that poem becomes a story. And every once in a while, those words take on an entire life of their own. That's exactly what happened while walking my favorite loop where cars are sparse and silence is abundant. What began with the words *the world needs* took me to a place unimagined and brought me back a changed person. Here is where it all started:

THE WORLD NEEDS

The world needs more patience.
Let it begin on the floor of my home as my child struggles to
    tie her own shoes before school.
The world needs more kindness.
Let it begin at my kitchen counter as I bite my tongue over
    spilled cereal and offer a helping hand.
The world needs more hope.
Let it begin on a piece of crisp, white stationery as I write
    words of encouragement for a hurting soul.

The world needs more peace.
Let it begin in my heart as I decide to pick my battles and
    say, "I am sorry," as often as I can.
The world needs more human connection.
Let it begin with my hands as I choose to hold on to my
    loved ones instead of my devices.
The world needs more compassion.
Let it begin with my feet as I walk in someone else's shoes
    instead of doling out judgment and contempt.
The world needs more patience, kindness, hope, peace,
    human connection, and compassion. Yes, it does. And the
    world is not too big, and these commodities are not too
    scarce.
It begins in our hearts, hands, words, and actions.
It begins with the people closest to us.
It begins with you and me.
It begins today.

As the poem reveals, I am a big believer in small, daily gestures of love. I believe such actions hold the power to transform our relationships, but also the world. So each day I try to make a difference by opening my arms to the ones closest to me. Most days, that is enough. Most days, that is more than enough. But then sometimes I am called to do more.

Sometimes I am asked to open my arms to those outside my inner circle. My first reaction is usually resistance, and that resistance can be very strong. Thoughts of time, cost, and inconvenience keep my arms tucked tightly around me. But I've learned something important on this Hands Free journey: when I feel most resistant to opening my arms is when I should open them the widest. So when my friend walked up to the church podium to talk about a mission God had placed on her heart, I secretly wished I hadn't come to church that day. My friend, who doesn't care for the spotlight or public recognition, was bravely holding a microphone telling the congregation about the calling she felt to redecorate the dark and gloomy rooms of a local women's shelter.

She explained that each of the one hundred rooms housed two mothers and their children who were trying to rebuild their lives after a traumatic life experience. My friend described how a little paint, some soft rugs, new towels, colorful bedding, and a bedside lamp could lift the women's spirits and make them feel worthy.

As this loving woman invited the congregation to adopt a room, I felt that familiar pang of resistance. I began calculating time, cost, effort, and availability. Just as I'd practically convinced myself I would pass on this opportunity, Natalie scooted up against me. Cupping my ear with her hand, she whispered enthusiastically, "Let's do it, Mom!"

Before I responded, I happened to look down at my arms. They were folded tightly around my body. I slowly opened them to pull my child close. The answer was clear. "Yes, Natalie," I agreed. "Let's do it." Then I said a prayer of gratitude, knowing my heart was about to be filled in unimaginable ways.

Natalie and I spent an afternoon shopping for items for the room makeover. I stuck to the practical things like a shower curtain and a trash can, but Natalie was drawn to items of comfort like candy, bags of coffee, soft blankets, and coconut-scented shampoo. I watched her arms fill with things that make a home a *home*.

On the day of the redecoration, we were joined by Natalie's and Avery's two best friends, Catherine and Meredith. I was amazed that there was no load too heavy ... no dirt stain too stubborn ... no bathroom bug too intimidating for these four kids. For six hours they cleaned, organized, and rearranged with vigor. At one point the children were folding baby clothes for the twins who lived in the room when a resident of the facility approached them. "You like helping people, don't you? I can tell," she said matter-of-factly.

After the resident walked away, I watched the children and thought about this unconventional compliment coming from someone who clearly had a different perspective about what actions were praiseworthy in society. She was definitely on to something, I thought. As I went back to scrubbing dirt off the linoleum floor, I expanded on her line of thinking:

What if emphasis was placed not on the price of our home, but on the openness of our hands? What if the warmth of our smile was noticed over the whiteness of our teeth? What if we acted on the callings of our hearts rather than mainstream media's materialistic urgings? What if our wealth was not measured by how much we possessed, but how much we gave?

Well, if the time my family and friends spent at the women's shelter was any indication, this would mean less competition, more compassion ... less greed, more gratitude ... less putting each other down, more holding each other up.

I wanted to be a part of this perspective shift in the world. It would start at home. I vowed to remember the powerful impact of outstretched arms despite my initial thoughts that almost discouraged me from helping. But just in case I needed one more confirmation, I received an email message from a mother of one of Natalie's classmates to seal my vow.

> Please tell Natalie thank you for me. I was tucking my child in bed and she was telling me about her day. She said they watched a movie in class and Natalie was the only one who let my daughter sit in her lap. She is our cuddly and nurturing child who feels safer when tucked in a lap, even at ten years old. She said that Natalie held her for the whole movie and that it was the best day because of that one thing.

If I didn't know it before, I knew it then: the world needs more open arms.

The children
The mamas
The daddies
The babies
The aging
The dying
The lonely
The sick
The weak

And even the strong . . .
They all need more open arms.

And we have them. We have them. Sometimes that is all that we have. But it is enough.

It is more than enough. Let us begin wherever we are.

HANDS FREE LIFE DAILY DECLARATION

Today I will look for those with warm smiles, helpful hands, and generous hearts. I will look for those who see hope where others see a hopeless cause. I will look for People Who Like to Help—those who replace fear, sorrow, and uncertainty with love, joy, and promise. They may never make the cover of a magazine, but they make the world a better place. Today I will tell them so, and I will act in kind. Instead of one set of open arms, there will be two. Instead of one positive spark, there will be two. Together, we can create an unstoppable light in a painfully dark world.

CHANGE SOMEONE'S STORY BY TAKING THE FIRST STEP

I was licking the envelope when Natalie came into the kitchen. "Who's the letter for?" she inquired. I told her it was for Miss Amanda, her former preschool teacher who had also been her babysitter when she was very young. Natalie didn't remember Miss Amanda, but I sure did. In fact, I would never forget her. There I was in a brand-new city with a baby, a toddler, and a traveling husband. Amanda would come to our house a few hours a week and play with Natalie and Avery. I remember feeling quite homesick and alone, yet incredibly grateful for this trustworthy young woman with gentle hands and a hearty laugh who was able to give me a reprieve.

"Amanda helped me through a very hard time when you and your sister were small," I explained. "And now, I want to help her.

203

She and her husband are trying to raise money to bring home their baby from Uganda."

"Can anyone help — or is it just for adults?" Natalie asked. When I told her anyone could donate, Natalie literally ran to get her wallet. She returned looking very sad. Much to her dismay, all that was left of her recent birthday money was one single dollar bill. Natalie didn't hide her look of anguish. "A dollar isn't much," she concluded sadly.

I held my breath. This child was my giver — the one who thought nothing of giving painted rocks or shiny seashells as birthday gifts or offering her own favorite trinkets to beloved friends. I would be heartbroken if she put the dollar back in her wallet, embarrassed to give such a small amount. I hoped societal influences hadn't already altered her uninhibited way of giving that had greatly impacted my own offerings.

"Do you think a dollar will make a difference?" Natalie asked skeptically.

I knew my answer had to be convincing. Just having turned double digits, Natalie was quite aware of what things cost — and I suspected she knew that adopting a baby was very costly. "Imagine if everyone Amanda knew gave one dollar," I proposed. Natalie could do the math. Her eyebrows rose with interest. "Plus, considering what she's going through, receiving a note of support from a child she used to babysit might mean even more to Amanda than money," I added.

Apparently, my response was sufficient. Natalie grabbed a notecard, jotted a message, inserted her dollar, and stuck the notecard in an envelope. After addressing it to Amanda with the information I provided, she carried it out to the mailbox.

A few weeks passed before we heard anything about the dollar donation. Surprisingly, Amanda posted the following message and photo of Natalie's handwritten note on a social media site:

> I received a sweet letter from a child I used to babysit. It said, "I hope that this helps adopt the child," and there was $1 included. It still brings tears to my eyes thinking about the compassion

in sweet Natalie's heart! If she only knew the difference she was making in people's lives! Because of her sweet gift, I want to see how many people would participate in Natalie's Dollar Challenge to "help adopt the child."

Extremely touched by Amanda's idea, I shared her photo with my friends and within just a few hours, Amanda wrote to inform me that $300 dollars had been raised. I printed Amanda's message and showed it to Natalie the next morning. "Remember when you asked if a dollar could make a difference?" I asked. "Take a look," I said, handing her the note.

As Natalie read Amanda's words, the most radiant smile appeared on her face. "Amanda is now three hundred steps closer to holding her baby in her arms," she said excitedly. As I watched my growing girl happily imagining a mother being united with her child, I suddenly felt an overwhelming peace about a worry that had haunted me for almost a decade.

When Natalie was six months old, one of her favorite activities was to be danced around the room by her daddy. Through her enthusiastic hand gestures, we learned that "Calling All Angels" by Train was her preferred dance song. When Scott would make angel wing motions with her little arms, Natalie would laugh hysterically. This, in turn, would make Scott and I laugh until we cried. Although I never spoke my true feelings aloud, inside I was dying. The lyrics of the song touched on every fear I was feeling as a new parent. The birth of Natalie had triggered an intense anguish within me about the state of the world. It seemed like the evening news was more disturbing than ever. It seemed like there were more child abductions, more bombings, more killings, more sadness, and more despair from the moment she arrived. *This is no place to raise a child*, I thought to myself several times a day — to the point that I wondered what kind of world Scott and I had brought our child into. As I held my sleeping baby, I often wondered if there would be any hope left in this world when she was an adult. I prayed that God would send angels to surround her with goodness as she grew.

And now, ten years later, I saw that he had. Standing in front of me was the hope I'd been looking for—I'd just been looking at it all wrong.

Angels were not divinely perfect beings dressed in billowy white gowns spreading goodwill just above our heads. Angels were imperfect human beings who lost their shoes several times a day, overindulged on chocolate milk, and got cranky when they didn't get enough sleep. Angels were freckle-faced darlings who dipped their steak in ketchup and absentmindedly left the car door open when they came home from swim practice. And if societal influences didn't get to them first, these pint-sized angels gave to others with no reservations and no inhibitions. If they saw someone who needed help, they helped. If they saw someone facing a mountainous challenge, they didn't see the impossible; they saw steps. And these earthly angels were willing to take the first one—even if it seemed small and insignificant.

The disheveled angel standing before me knew hope didn't come in the form of six-figure checks or expensive packages with gold bows. She knew hope came in handwritten notes with misplaced commas and poor penmanship. She knew hope came in the form of small, loving gestures that inspired others to act in kind. In one definitive moment, ten years' worth of fear subsided, and my hope for the future swelled. All at once, the world didn't look so bleak for my child who looked more and more like she needed me less and less. As long as a child's single dollar bill could bring a loving couple three hundred steps closer to bringing their baby home, there was hope. I gathered my living, breathing angel into my arms and recited a prayer. It went something like this:

Dear God,

Let me not get caught up in the dangers of the world that are beyond my control. Let me refuse to believe there is nothing I can do to bring goodness to a troubled and complicated world. Let me reject societal influences that try to influence how much I give, what I give, or whom I give it to. If in this sometimes dark and hurting world a ten-year-old child with skinned knees and overgrown toenails can be an angel, then there is hope for us all. Let me give as my child gives. Let me remember nothing is too small. Let me not give up the good fight. Amen.

Within six short months of Natalie placing a dollar in an envelope, a little boy was brought home from a Ugandan orphanage. Like Natalie, there were others who believed a dollar could make a difference, and they put that belief into action by sending their own dollar bills to a couple longing for a child to call their own. As a result, a little boy named Jac who had never smiled much during the first two years of his life came to smile nearly all the time, especially when he looked at his mother, Miss Amanda. I cannot be certain, but whenever Jac says, "I ov wu, Mama," I believe that is when the angels sing—from the back of the school bus or with a hairbrush in front of the bathroom mirror. Every time I hear those angelic voices drifting through my home, I am reminded that love can transform broken hearts and transcend dismal situations when one person, big or small, believes that it can.

 ## HANDS FREE LIFE DAILY DECLARATION

There will come a day when my loved ones have to brave the world. I do not want to send them into uncharted territory without preparing and equipping them for what they may face. Therefore, my daily vow is to give my loved ones many pieces of protective armor that will help them carry on, make sound decisions, and guard their heart. This internal armor shall come from daily offerings of presence, wisdom, faith, and unconditional love. I shall not worry about worldly harm that is beyond my control. I shall focus on what I can control—contributing peace, hope, and stability to the world by loving the people with whom I share my life.

HANDS FREE LIFE HABIT BUILDER 9

Change Someone's Story with the Six-Second Challenge

In 6 seconds you can kiss someone like you mean it.

In 6 seconds you can hold open a door.

In 6 seconds you can wait for a little straggler to catch up. "I'll wait for you," you can even say.

In 6 seconds you can take a deep breath.

In 6 seconds you can let it go. "It's not worth it," you can say.

In 6 seconds you can tuck a note in a lunch box or in a pocket. It takes 2 seconds to draw a heart.

In 6 seconds you can say you're sorry.

In 6 seconds you can cut yourself some slack.

In 6 seconds you can throw away that picture, that pair of pants, that inner bully that keeps you from loving this day, this you.

In 6 seconds you can feel the sunshine.

In 6 seconds you can decide it's time to stop looking back.

In 6 seconds you can whisper, "It's gonna be okay" to yourself or someone who's scared.

In 6 seconds you can drop a dollar in a hat.

In 6 seconds you can pick up that old guitar.

In 6 seconds you can look into someone's eyes and say, "My life is better because of you."

I used to sound like a broken record. "I don't have time," I would always say.

But then I discovered what could happen in a mere 6 seconds.

It's enough to make a bad day good . . .

It's enough to bring life back to your weary bones . . .

It's enough to remember what really matters in the midst of so much
that doesn't . . .
It's enough to change someone's story
and send a ripple of unending kindness and love out into the world.

It doesn't take much to change someone's story. In fact, six seconds
will do. I wrote "The Six-Second Challenge" while waiting for Banjo the cat
at the emergency vet clinic. A few days before, I'd accidentally discovered it
took six seconds for Banjo to start purring whenever I picked him up. This
discovery inspired me to look for other ways I could offer love to other living
beings or myself in a mere six seconds. Much to my surprise, there were
countless ways to impact someone's day, yet the impact of that action
lasted far longer. What can you do in six seconds to change someone's
story or at least make it a little brighter? I guarantee that just trying to find
out will bring you joy and make the world a better place for everyone.

CONCLUSION

May you live all the days of your life.

Jonathan Swift

I DUG AROUND IN my purse until I found the bright orange paper containing directions to a local retirement home. As I read the steps out loud to Scott while he drove, I felt a sense of peace about where we were heading. The list of project sites for the Magic City Miracle community service day had been extensive, but the decision to visit the elderly had been a unanimous decision for our family. I did have one regret, though. I wished I'd thought to bring one of my pocket-size writing notebooks that I typically carried in case something happened that I didn't want to forget.

I didn't have my notebook that day, but I managed to mentally collect more than a dozen poignant moments that began on the car ride to the facility and ended as I pulled the covers up to my daughter's chin. Like the deep crevices that lined the worn hands we held that day, these moments are engrained in my mind indefinitely.

I won't forget how, on the way to the retirement home, Natalie told Avery that she googled what to say to senior citizens. From the backseat I heard, "A safe question is 'What is your favorite memory?' But don't ask, 'How old are you?'"

I won't forget how my daughters stared out the car windows clutching bags of handmade cards, their hopeful faces indicating they were eager to distribute messages of love. "Breathe in blue sky, breathe out gray sky," said one card in the most delicate font I'd seen written by a child.

I won't forget how neither an ominous security system nor a strong medicinal odor deterred the children from eagerly walking through the double doors to meet those eagerly waiting on the other side.

I won't forget how my daughters and their friends walked right up to the wheelchair bound, refusing to allow bulky walkers to impede their ability to get close to those who needed closeness.

I won't forget how the mere sight of smiley, disheveled children made dull eyes light up and lowly hung heads rise.

I won't forget the woman in the lavender sweater. Her words were so soft and so shaky that I struggled to understand. Yet Natalie walked up and began nodding her head as if she understood every word.

I won't forget watching Avery read her homemade card to a silver-haired woman in a tattered sweater. I won't forget how despite having severely hunched shoulders and being nonverbal, the woman leaned forward gracefully and kissed Avery on the forehead. I won't forget how Avery's face brightened, as if blessed by a royal queen.

I won't forget how Avery summoned me into a resident's room. "Mama, you just have to come see," she whispered. And when I entered, I gasped at the dismal sight of a bone-thin woman in sheer pajamas lying in a bed with an oxygen mask hooked to her face. I won't forget how I recoiled, thinking of my grandma in her darkest days. I won't forget how my feet wouldn't move, but Avery's hand reached for mine. "C'mon, Mama," she coaxed. "Meet my friend. She's very nice."

I won't forget how Natalie broke the silence of a somber hallway with lightning-fast feet and celebratory words. "You've *got* to come to Mrs. Bonnie's room. She's one hundred! She's one hundred!" Natalie exclaimed as she motioned me forward.

I won't forget how a group of children had gathered around a beautiful lady wearing a bright yellow sweater and a shy smile.

Mrs. Bonnie had recently turned one hundred years old, but she was as spry as someone half her age. I won't forget how Bonnie's eighty-eight-year-old roommate called Bonnie "Mom" and how the two held hands for a picture.

I won't forget how the residents cried when it was time for us to go.

I won't forget how the children hugged their white-haired friends and said, "We'll be back soon. Next time, we'll bring candy!"

I won't forget how the woman in pink called out, "I hope I'm still here."

I won't forget how I wanted to blurt out the same exact words, but with one added detail. "I hope I'm still here too," I wanted to rejoice at the top of my lungs. "I hope to live a very long time! I'm *keeping track of life*, you know!"

No one would've known what I was talking about, except maybe Avery. She'd given me that term, *keeping track of life*, which helped me distinguish which numbers, efforts, achievements, commitments, and opinions mattered from the ones that didn't. Being in the nursing home that day must have triggered the same thoughts of dying, living, and *keeping track of life* in Avery's mind as it did in mine. As I was tucking her into bed that night, Avery asked when we'd be going back to the retirement home to see the people in "wheely chairs."

I told Avery that the director of the nursing home had given me her contact information and suggested we come back for the holidays. Then I crawled into the bed to read to her like I did every night. Except this time, Avery felt like talking.

"What do you think you would be doing right now if you didn't start being a Hands Free mama?"

The question stunned me. I could not find any words. I attempted to swallow the emotion welling up inside my throat.

"Well, I know," she volunteered. "You wouldn't be here with me. You would be too busy to spend time with me and Natalie. You would not laugh very much. And you wouldn't be you."

I reached out and held her. There was really no more to say even if I *could* speak. *I would not be me.* Someday, when Avery could fully understand, I would tell her how true that statement was. I would not be...

that squeaky violin player,
that sandy-footed starfish rescuer,
that notebook-filling author,
that peaceful graveyard visitor,
that observant Noticer-in-training,
that open-armed giver,
that patient encourager,
that two-handed hugger.
that authentically messy, lovingly flawed lover of life.

In my pursuit of a Hands Free Life, I'd found beloved parts of myself that I'd thought were gone and even some parts I didn't know existed. What parts of me were yet to be discovered, cultivated, and set free? The possibilities made me want to jump for joy and continue living Hands Free till the ripe old age of one hundred like Mrs. Bonnie. Perhaps someday kind people would visit me in the nursing home and be enamored by the twinkle in my eye.

"Did you see her sparkle? I wonder where it came from," I could imagine the visitors whispering as they left me for my afternoon nap. I would smile from my plush recliner, wishing that everyone knew the secret to the sparkle was really no secret at all. It was merely evidence of a life well lived:

I made someone smile.
I gave a tender kiss.
I hugged and wasn't the first to let go.
I encouraged.
I laughed.
I believed.
I lifted.
I kneeled.

I forgave.

I loved.

I kept track of life.

And in doing so, I found that the most important things in life are not measured but are felt through the hands, heart, and soul of each life we touch.

But most importantly, I hoped everyone knew, as it is written in this book, a *life* well lived began with a *minute*, an *hour*, a single *day* well lived.

So let us begin right now.

Let us feed our sparkle and light up our life.

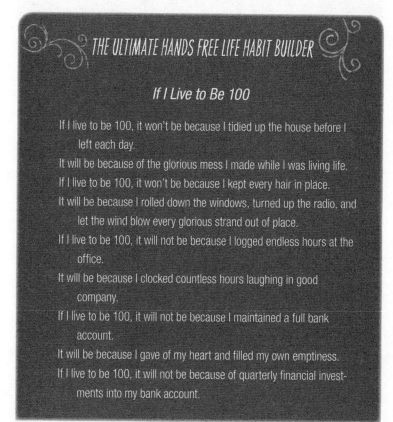

THE ULTIMATE HANDS FREE LIFE HABIT BUILDER

If I Live to Be 100

If I live to be 100, it won't be because I tidied up the house before I left each day.

It will be because of the glorious mess I made while I was living life.

If I live to be 100, it won't be because I kept every hair in place.

It will be because I rolled down the windows, turned up the radio, and let the wind blow every glorious strand out of place.

If I live to be 100, it will not be because I logged endless hours at the office.

It will be because I clocked countless hours laughing in good company.

If I live to be 100, it will not be because I maintained a full bank account.

It will be because I gave of my heart and filled my own emptiness.

If I live to be 100, it will not be because of quarterly financial investments into my bank account.

It will be because of daily emotional investments into my most sacred
relationships.

If I live to be 100, it will not be because I separated myself from the
sick and the weak.

It will be because I walked right up to suffering and lovingly reached
out my hand.

If I live to be 100, it will not be because I could accomplish more in
one day than most could in a week.

It will be because I took time to gaze at stars, sip hot chocolate, and
walk *beside* my children, not ahead of them.

If I live to be 100, it will not be because I earned prestigious degrees
that lined my walls.

It will be because I pursued the passions of my heart and decorated
my soul.

If I live to be 100, it will not be because I used expensive efforts to
prevent aging.

It will be because I embraced my wrinkles, took walks, and left all
regrets in the past.

If I live to be 100, it will be because

I listened more than I spoke,

I leaned in for kisses,

I cried with those who cried,

I recognized my blessings,

I kept my promises,

I gave loving hellos and undistracted goodbyes.

If I live to be 100, it will be because I lived and loved

more than my heart ever thought possible.

ACKNOWLEDGMENTS

THE WRITING OF THIS book occurred during a time of transition for my family. My familiar sources of encouragement, support, and inspiration that used to fuel my writing in the past were disrupted by an out-of-state move. For many weeks I felt lost, homesick, and worried that I would not meet the deadline for submitting this book to my publisher. For the first time in my life I found it difficult to write, so I stopped. I stopped trying and let myself acclimate to my new surroundings. I put my complete trust in God that this book would be written in his time. Six weeks later, this book flowed from my fingertips. The night before, Scott had taken me to see one of my favorite bands, Counting Crows, at an intimate outdoor venue. The first song the band performed was a rendition of "Round Here" that was unlike anything I'd ever heard. As Adam Duritz invited us to climb outside the figurative windows of our lives, tears streamed down my face. The lyrics, in conjunction with the beautiful melody, made me want to live ... love ... dream ... forgive ... embrace ... create ... heal ... grow. The way the song made me feel about living life was exactly what I wanted people to feel when they read my book. At last, I had a concrete goal: Write words that ignite a sense of urgency to live freely and love fully despite the distractions, reservations, and fears that divert us from our path. I am eternally grateful for that life-altering moment that provided direction and inspiration for this book.

So in the spirit of *moments that inspired this book*, I offer these acknowledgements:

Sandra Bishop, I am grateful for the moment we came up with the perfect subtitle for this book. It was not the one that was used—and I couldn't even tell you what that one was now—but that was the moment I knew we'd be a *forever team*. That was the moment I knew you understood my heart … my passion … my calling like no one else could. You support my dreams. You listen to my nightmares. You have my back. You are not simply my literary agent—you are my friend, my interpreter, my confidant, my protector, my warrior. You were providentially appointed to help me carry out my life's purpose. Wherever you go, I will go with you.

Rebecca Macy, I am grateful for the moment we were trying to get out the door during your summer visit and I fell apart. Although I did not say I was stressed about meeting the deadline for this book, you knew exactly why I was troubled. You said, "How can I help?" Those were your words. They have always been your words, my big sister, who is always there to lift, encourage, and believe in me. This book and the one before it would not be in existence without the lifelong support and helpfulness you have offered and provided.

Eleanor Williams, I am grateful for the moment we walked up that Alabama hill one last time together and you shared the advice you'd given Gibs the night before: "Look for the blessings—you might not see them right away, but just keep looking. Keep looking for the blessings." I held on to those words like a security blanket and used them more times than I could count while adjusting to a new place with new people and new experiences. Your beautiful Southern voice is so often in my head, reminding me to call the grocery store employees by name and to go to battle for those who cannot go to battle for themselves. Your wisdoms are forever in my heart, and they undoubtedly made their way into this book.

James Harbour, at my first-ever book signing you sat on the floor in the front row. Your eager, smiling face was my focal point. I will never forget the moment I spoke of my dream because that is when I caught a glimpse of your dream. The way your eyes lit up when I encouraged the crowd to pursue the urgings of their hearts stirred something inside me. In that moment, I yearned to write a children's book that would inspire young people to shine their Firefly Light. I pray my dream comes to fruition along with yours, James. And to your precious family: I never knew what that light next door meant to me until it was no longer there. Jennifer, Jim, James, and Lauren, thank you for being that constant source of light in darkness. Even from a distance, I can still see it and feel it.

Pastor Wade Griffith, I am grateful for that moment you allowed Natalie to tell the congregation about Pricilla ... that moment you asked Scott to join the UMCOR Early Response Team to aid the tornado survivors in Tuscaloosa ... that moment you believed our church could pull off the Magic City Miracle ... that moment you celebrated five thousand packed shoeboxes for Operation Christmas Child and shared the news that one person really can make a difference. This book, as well as my heart, would have gigantic holes in it had it not been for the profound opportunities you and Liberty Crossings United Methodist Church provided our family to be a blessing.

Carolyn McCready, I am grateful for the moment you sat on the back patio with my children as they delighted in you just as I did the first time I met you. I can mark that gorgeous fall evening as the first time my new home felt like home. There you were, raving about the first draft of this book, talking about future projects, and allowing me to describe some of the hurts and fears that come with this work I've been called to do. Carolyn, when I hand my words over to you, I know they could not be in better care. Thank you for trusting my vision, my instincts, my choices, and for allowing me to soar under your loving guidance.

Along with those moments, there were also these constants that allowed this book to be written:

To my incredible team at HarperCollins Christian Publishing/ Zondervan/Choice Publicity: Carolyn McCready, Londa Alderink, Bob Hudson, Heather Adams, Beth Gebhard, Kristin Carver, and Jennifer VerHage. Each one of you has a special way of building me up, preparing me for the unknown, and spreading the Hands Free message so it can reach those who need it most. Thank you for loving me despite my imperfections and insecurities. Thank you for continually praying for me and my family's safety and well-being. Thank you for believing.

To Beth Berutich and Shannon Brooks: Thank you for listening to God's calling on your heart to change lives through Innocence Lost and the Lovelady Center. This book would not be what it is without your influence, your inspiration, and your tremendous support of my work. I aspire to have a listening heart like yours.

To Scott's immediate and extended family: Thank you for enveloping me in the love of a big family. You are people who give the tightest hugs, load the counters with delicious food, and welcome all to the table. You are people who never waste an opportunity to say, "I love you" and know the priceless value of state-fair visits, fishing at the pond, and Uncle Tackle Time. Thank you for always having my back when haters on the Internet and in the movie ticket line try to bring me down. Thank you for coming out in full force to book signings and sharing my work with anyone who will listen. The way you live, love, and remember loved ones who have gone before us greatly influenced my writing in chapter 8.

To Stacie and Jon Oliver: Thank you for allowing your home to become *The Hands Free Shop* where my dream of tangible reminders to live better and love more came to fruition. Stacie, you manage the shop like a boss. With your loving touches on every product and every shipment, you make so many people happy (well, except when the "Only Love Today" bracelets sell out). Stacie and Jon, thank you for consulting with me on the cover of this book until it matched what I envisioned in my mind ... for being the best Hands Free parents I have ever known ... for allowing me to hear the blessed words "Aunt Rachel" spoken by Sam, Evan, and Kate. You have given me a chance to relive some of the precious moments I missed before I knew how to truly live.

Kristin Shaw, Don Blackwell, and Lisa McCrohan: I am not sure how you know, but you always know when my spirit needs lifting. Several times throughout the process of writing this book, your words of encouragement carried me. As writers who know the pros and cons of sharing one's heart with the world, your understanding is often enough to carry me through.

Christi McGuire, Katie Mohr, and Katrina Willis: The words in this book would not be what they are without your brilliance, your expertise, and your guidance. You help me find the words when I am having trouble doing so. But above of all, thank you for knowing my heart. The whole world could be against me and yet you would stand beside me and say, "I'm with her." Do you know what that kind of belief and loyalty does for me? It allows me to write down the hard stuff and hit publish. Thank you for standing beside me so I can lean on you whenever I falter.

Mary Largent, Jennifer Harbour, Shannon Brooks, Carrie Wertheimer, Julia Griffith, and Kellie McIntyre: your faithful friendship and sisterly love provided strength in the writing of this book more times than I can count. Thank you for missing me, lifting me, walking with me, being happy with me, being sad with me, praying for me, asking me to pray for you, reading my words, sharing my words, but most of all, thank you for being real so I can be real too.

Coach Tavie, Coach Amy, Coach Jennifer, and Coach Katie: Thank you for building my children up, giving them room to grow, and allowing them to be who they are. Thank you for standing behind the block with an unlimited supply of patience and encouragement. Without the experiences from the YMCA pool, this book would be lacking. What I learned from you about patience, presence, and stepping back has changed the course of my daughters' lives in the most positive way.

Andrew Henderson: Thank you for seeing the light in our Firefly and cultivating that light with your gentle teachings and extraordinary talent. You showed me what calmness and positivity can do for a little girl trying to learn something new. The impact of your presence on Avery's confidence and ability to shine her unique light has been profound. I am grateful for your contribution to this book and to her life.

To Nancy Janas and Kristi Seigel: your beautiful, giving hearts that reached out to our family when we knew no one provided the perfect beginning to our new life and the perfect ending to this book. God gave us you.

To Sandy Blackard and Dr. Theresa Kellam: Thank you for helping me answer the toughest, most painful questions posed by readers of my blog. Your willingness to help those you have never met without asking for anything in return is truly remarkable and generous. Through your brilliant responses, I have learned a great deal about communicating with compassion and creating a loving, peaceful home.

To *The Hands Free Revolution* community and beloved readers of my blog: During the writing of this book, I relied heavily on your messages of gratitude and support. Through your comments, I experienced divine fuel and affirmation. Through your questions, I felt an urgency to get this book into your hands. Thank you for allowing me to be human ... for coming to my defense ... for sharing my messages with others. Your presence is a daily blessing that moves me like nothing I've ever known. You often say, "Please never stop writing!" My request to you is: please never stop walking beside me on this journey.

And to my greatest constants ...

To my parents, Harry and Delpha: your influence on my life, my writing, and my parenting is evident on every page of this book. Thank you for guiding, believing, encouraging, reading, editing, caregiving, and supporting me throughout my entire life and during the writing of this book. Above all, thank you for listening. My joys and successes on this journey are not joys and successes until they are shared with you. I have learned that listening is love through your consistent desire to hear what I have to say. Mom and Dad, I was able to write about building up a human being in this book because of you.

To Natalie: our relationship is my daily motivation for living Hands Free. The way you talk to me and confide in me inspires me to be *all there* despite the distractions of life. I never want to miss one of your questions, one of your amazing insights, or one of your hand squeezes. Thank you for saying and believing "Mama always comes." It is the greatest compliment I have ever been given. I pray each day to be the One Who Always Comes no matter what life throws my way. Natalie, I was able to write about the gift of unconditional presence in this book because of you.

To Avery: every day in your company is a lesson in living a joy-filled life. My daily goal is to approach each moment, each day, and each human being the way you do—with a welcoming smile, with genuine enthusiasm, and with selfless love. Thank you for freely giving me what I often lack. When I lose my zest, you are my cheer. When I feel guilt, you are my grace. When I am rushed, you are my pause. When I lose perspective, you are my eyes. Avery, I was able to write about being a Lover of Life in this book because of you.

To Scott: I know that whether I have one reader or one million readers, whether I have a bestseller or a dud, whether I write ten more books or none, you will love me. You love me without conditions and restraint. You love me because I am me. You love me as is, and that love has changed me for the better. When I heard "only love today" silence my inner bully, it was your voice I heard. Thank you for never failing to comfort me after a bad dream. Thank you for never failing to look out for my health and well-being. Scott, I was able to write about unconditional love in this book because of you.

Dear God: Procrastination, distraction, and fear lose their power when a heart decides what it must do before it stops beating. You revealed this to me as I neared the conclusion of chapter 6. I am so thankful I lived to write this. I am so thankful I wrote to live this. Thank you for choosing me to be your messenger. I shall write for you, dear Lord, until the very last beat of my heart.

Hands Free Mama

A Guide to Putting Down the
Phone, Burning the To-Do List,
and Letting Go of Perfection to
Grasp What Really Matters!

Rachel Macy Stafford

*Rachel Macy Stafford's post "The Day I
Stopped Saying Hurry Up" was a true phe-
nomenon on The Huffington Post, igniting
countless conversations online and off about freeing ourselves from
the vicious cycle of keeping up with our overstuffed agendas. Hands
Free Mama has the power to keep that conversation going and remind
us that we must not let our lives pass us by.*

—**Arianna Huffington**, Chair, President, and Editor-in-Chief of the Huffington
Post Media Group, nationally syndicated columnist, and author of thirteen
books http://www.huffingtonpost.com/

DISCOVER THE POWER, JOY, AND LOVE of Living "Hands Free"

In 2010, special-education teacher and mother Rachel Macy Stafford
decided enough was enough. Tired of losing track of what matters most
in life, Rachel began practicing simple strategies that enabled her to let go
of largely meaningless distractions and engage in meaningful soul-to-soul
connections. She started a blog to chronicle her endeavors and soon saw
how both external and internal distractions had been sabotaging her happiness and preventing her from bonding with the people she loves most.

Hands Free Mama is the digital society's answer to finding balance in a
media-saturated, perfection-obsessed world. It doesn't mean giving up all
technology forever. It doesn't mean forgoing our jobs and responsibilities.
What it does mean is looking our loved ones in the eye and giving them
the gift of our undivided attention, leaving the laundry till later to dance
with our kids in the rain, and living a present, authentic, and intentional life
despite a world full of distractions.

So join Rachel and go hands-free. Discover what happens when you
choose to open your heart—and your hands—to each God-given moment.

Available in stores and online!